MW00892419

Living Life in the Kingdom

Lessons from the Throne Room of God

Joanne M. Green

Published by Purpose Publishing LLC.
1503 Main Street #168 ❧ Grandview, Missouri
www.purposepublishing.com

ISBN: 978-09861063-9-2

Copyright © 2016 Joanne M. Green
Cover design by: Riyana Arts
Editing by Team Green

Printed in the United States of America

Dedication

This book is dedicated to Pastor Connie McGrue and the Prayer-Warriors4life Ministry. Pastor Connie has been so gracious to allow me to share these lessons as part of her national online bible study.

I would also like to dedicate this book to a true Prayer-Warrior4life and dear friend, Pastor Maxine Goodrich who has joined the "great cloud of witnesses" and is now looking over the bannister of Heaven to cheer us all on...Love you Pastor Max.

Table of Contents

Section 1
The Person of the Holy Spirit

Section 2
The Holy Spirit's Gifts to You

Section 3
Identifying Your Motivational Gifts

Section 4
The Fruits of Character

Section 5
Motivational Gift Assessment Survey

- Plan of salvation
- baptism of the Holy Spirit
- growth plan to operate in their spiritual gifts

Spiritual Gifts
I Corinthians 12:1-11

     Wisdom
     Knowledge
     faith
gifts of healing
working of miracles
     prophecy
ability to distinguish between spirits
various kinds of tongues
interpretation of tongues

The Spirit gives gifts, which believers use to serve Christ, and the Father produces results.

Foreword

Kingdom Principles

You are picking up this book because the title caught your attention and you are reading this page because you have an interest in "Living Life in the Kingdom." Joanne has allowed God to use her to create this "must have" tool for every leader's training arsenal. She has done a phenomenal job of articulating the plan of salvation, baptism of the Holy Spirit and the growth plan for anyone to operate within their spiritual gifts.

After over seventy years of working in ministry, I can honestly say that the teachings in this book masterfully detail Kingdom principles I have applied and brought to my attention principles I had missed. This manual provides structure and gives language to principles and strategies that God anointed me to implement in ministry. Like me, I believe you are going to immediately recognize areas she shares and say, "oh yes, I have done this before but not in a structured format." As the Founder of Center of Hope Community Church and Kingdom Builders Ministerial Alliance, as well as Founder of several building projects that include a 150 unit affordable housing complex, a 56 unit senior housing building, and a 17-unit transitional facility for homeless single women with children and as an Author and Mentor to many men and women from all walks of life, I recommend and endorse the information shared in this manual.

I was fortunate to meet Joanne many years ago and I have been blessed by her profound ability to teach complex biblical information with a practical application to **live life in the Kingdom** on a daily basis. This manual offers scriptural based and detailed teachings on: The Person of the Holy Spirit, The Holy Spirit's Gift to You, Identifying Your Motivational Gifts and The Fruits of Character. This kind of practical teaching is so vital and needful in our churches today. We need organized methods to quickly capture the attention of our diverse congregations and it is why I believe the information outlined in this manual truly delivers on meeting those needs. I admonish you to use this manual as another tool to help you and others identify your gifts, as well as understand and appreciate each member in the body of Christ and how all are fitly joined together to supply one another.

As a former Associate Pastor, Author, Bible Teacher and Speaker Joanne travels extensively sharing the Word of God. Her teaching is so engaging and inspiring as she challenges you to be honest about your own Christian walk. I am confident this new resource tool will assist you in counseling individuals and encourage families to strive to serve God at their highest and best level ensuring healthy spiritual growth. I endorse and highly recommend **"Living Life in the Kingdom "**.

-Bishop Ernestine Cleveland Reems, Oakland, California

Founder, Center of Hope Church

Founder, Kingdom Builders Ministerial Alliance

- identify your gifts
- understand & appreciate others
- how we are joined together to supply one another

Introduction

The Holy Spirit often gets overlooked as to the role He plays in the life of mankind and the new believer. He is very much a part of the Godhead as is the Father and Jesus. The Holy Spirit was not only seen in the book of Genesis but we can find evidence of Him throughout the Old Testament as well as the New Testament scriptures.

Nothing was given life apart from His breath or His Presence. It is with this revelation that these lessons from the Throne Room of God found their beginning. **Ruach Hakodesh** as He is called by the Jewish people reveals Himself in ways that will astound you and give you a lens in which to see depths of the Father that will draw you to a more intimate relationship with Adonai our Sovereign Lord and King.

↳ God is the Lord of all humanity; "Lord of all Lords"

This will be a journey for some and a revisiting of an old familiar place for others but all will be inspired to grasp the new experience of revelation unearthed by **Ruach Hakodesh.** But, as the Tanakh (Torah or Hebrew Teachings) says, *9 "No eye has seen, no ear has heard and no one's heart has imagined all the things that God has prepared for those who love him." 10 It is to us, however, that God has revealed these things. How? Through the Spirit. For the Spirit probes all things, even the profoundest depths of God. 11 For who knows the inner workings of a person except the person's own spirit inside him? So too no one knows the inner workings of God except God's Spirit.* **2 Corinthians 2:9-11.**

The Holy Spirits gifts to you are given to be utilized and have an impact in the kingdom of God. But first they must be identified.

Identifying your motivational gifts are available to every member of the body of Christ. But we need to know how they fit within the contexts of the body. Operating within the context of the kingdom will add value to your life and the lives of those you touch.

The Fruits of Character need to be on display for others to know who you are within and as well as who you are outside of the body of Christ. Integrity is a missing virtue in our society today and we desperately need to develop self-discipline that is built on the fruits of unconditional love, kindness and patience. If we live by the Spirit and allow His Spirit to live in us, then our lives will conform and align to the character of Christ! Get ready for an adventuresome spiritual journey to fulfill your ultimate call here on earth.

Walking in the Spirit; being led by the Spirit

Section 1

THE PERSON OF THE HOLY SPIRIT

Lesson 1

The Holy Spirit in the beginning

I know that it is clear to us that everything we see in the earth realm now or in the past has an origin. But what has not been made very clear is that God never acted alone. His work of Creation reveals to us that He worked in perfect union and harmony with Himself. In the beginning God reveals to us all of who He is by the following scriptures:

Genesis 1:1 *states that in the beginning God created the heavens and the earth. 2 The earth was without form, and void; and darkness was on the face of the deep. And the Spirit of God was hovering over the face of the waters. This is the first mention of the personage of the Holy Spirit.*

Question: What was the Holy Spirit doing?
Answer: He was hovering or brooding over the earth.

To **hover** means to hang fluttering or suspended in the air, to keep lingering about.
To **brood** means to cover, to loom, to fill the atmosphere or to breed.
To **breed** means to produce, procreate.

In other words, the **Holy Spirit** was preparing the earth for creation to bring forth life. This would be accomplished by reproducing what God spoke through controlled pollination in the environment. The **Holy Spirit** would also impart Life into the soul of the first man Adam.

He is the third person in the Trinity. **Genesis 1:26** states *Then God said, "Let Us make man in Our image according to Our likeness; let them have dominion over the fish of the sea, over the birds of the air, and over the cattle, over all the earth and over every creeping thing that creeps on the earth." 27 So God created man in His own image; in the image of God He* *created him; male and female He created them. It is here, that we notice God is not acting alone in creating His creation and its inhabitants. Christians therefore believe in the existence of the Trinity or Godhead.*

Genesis 2: 7 *And the Lord God formed man of the dust of the ground, and breathed into his nostrils the breath of life; and man became a living being.* **This is the work of the Holy Spirit**.

- Let's look at some examples of Him at work in scripture.

Luke 1:30 *Then the angel said to her, "Do not be afraid, Mary, for you have found favor with God. 31 And behold, **you will conceive in your womb** **and bring forth a Son, and shall call His name Jesus. 34** Then Mary said to the angel, "How can this be, since I do not know a man?" 35 And the angel answered and said to her, "**The Holy Spirit will come upon you, and the** **power of the Highest will overshadow you**; therefore, also, that Holy One who is to be born will be called the Son of God.*

This was much like what took place in the beginning when the Holy Spirit was brooding over the earth and gave life to the human soul of Adam. He broods over Mary's womb and gives "Life" to the seed of the Father that was planted. This is why some refer to the birth of Jesus Christ as an incarnate birth. Mary was a virgin but the seed of Jesus was placed in her womb.

- Another example of the Holy Spirit coming upon man.

Exodus 31:3-6 Then the Lord spoke to Moses, saying: **2** *"See, I have called by name Bezalel the son of Uri, the son of Hur, of the tribe of Judah. 3 And **I have filled him with the Spirit of God**, in wisdom, in understanding, in knowledge, and in all manner of workmanship, 4 to design artistic works, to work in gold, in silver, in bronze, 5 in cutting jewels for setting, in carving wood, and to work in all manner of workmanship. 6 And I, indeed I, have appointed with him Aholiab the son of Ahisamach, of the tribe of Dan; and I have put wisdom in the hearts of all*

who are gifted artisans, that they may make all that I have commanded you.
They were given the ability to create!

They were filled in measure not in fullness (as believers in Christ are today). They were empowered by the **Holy Spirit** to know and understand the laws or techniques about construction in order to build the tabernacle God had commanded them to construct. The tabernacle had many intricate and complex furnishing and it would take the help of the **Holy Spirit** to bring them to an understanding as how to build according to God's design. This is another indication to us that God intended for us to work with the **Holy Spirit** in the earth in order to accomplish "greater works". The tabernacle was being constructed so that **God – Elohim (the Father, Son and Holy Spirit)** could reside in their midst, much like what he established with Adam before the fall, when He came down to fellowship with Adam and Eve in the cool of the day.

Question: What have we established? GOD
God is in union with Himself to Create, **He is the Creator**; to Speak, **He is the Word** and to give life or Empower, **He is the Holy Spirit.**
JESUS   HOLY SPIRIT
The Creator spoke the Word, (Jesus is the Word). John 1, says In the beginning was the Word and the Word was with God and the Word was God. The same was in the beginning **with God**. Life was formed in the earth because the Holy Spirit gave Life to what was created.

This union is called the Divine Trinity or Holy Trinity:

Reference Scriptures:
1 John 5: 7 *For there are three that bear witness in heaven: the Father, the Word, and the Holy Spirit; and these three are one.*

Genesis 11: 6, 7 *And the Lord said, "Indeed the people are one and they all have one language, and this is what they begin to do; now nothing that they* *propose to do will be withheld from them. 7 Come, let Us go down and there confuse their language, that they may not understand one another's speech."*

Our study, as we move through these lessons will focus solely on The **Holy Spirit, Ruach Hakodesh** and His function in the believer's life. Ruach Hakodesh is the Hebrew word for Holy Spirit and is used in Jewish scripture to describe Him. Ruach meaning breath, air or wind of God.

The **Holy Spirit, Ruach Hakodesh** is referred to as our Helper and The Spirit of Truth in **John 14:16, 17** *And I will pray the Father, and He will give you another Helper, that He may abide with you forever. 17 The Spirit of Truth, whom the world cannot receive, because it neither sees Him nor knows Him; but you know Him, for He dwells with you and will be in you.*

The **Holy Spirit, Ruach Hakodesh** is our Counselor mentioned in **John 14:25, 26** *"These things I have spoken to you while being present with you. 26 But the Helper, Ruach Hakodesh whom the Father will send in My name, He will teach you all things, and bring to your remembrance all things that I said to you.*

[handwritten note:] Ruach Hakodesh = Holy Spirit → Helper / Spirit of Truth / Counselor / Breath, air, wind of God

Lesson 2

The Person of the Holy Spirit

We have established that the **Holy Spirit, Ruach Hakodesh is the third person of the Godhead/Trinity and He was revealed** in creation when He gave life to the earth and life to mankind. We should also note He gives not only physical life but spiritual life.

That's right, God spoke to the earth and "life" appeared, life was visible. Everything that God spoke the **Holy Spirit, Ruach Hakodesh** had **already prepared** the earth to bring forth.

<u>Prophetically Speaking</u>- The Holy Spirit has already "prepared some of our circumstances to bring forth". He has been hovering over our circumstances and situations to begin cultivating areas in those dark and empty places to bring about LIFE! What looks like nothingness is only a covering to protect what will be brought forth. This is like what the mother's placenta is to her unborn child in that it provides protection and nourishment to sustain life and removes everything that is toxic or harmful. That nothingness, that dark void space that you are seeing or sensing is like a placenta. God has placed a protective layer over you that has everything necessary to bring forth life and to remove anything and everything that has been toxic or harmful to your existence. God's release of resources will begin to flow into those circumstances and areas void of life. If it is lack, know that abundance is about to come forth; if it is sickness or disease, know that health and healing is coming forth; if it has been unemployment know that doors of opportunity are about to be opened that no one can keep closed or prevent from being opened to you. There is a relationship that looks like it is going nowhere, hold on, that relationship is about to change from a lack of commitment to total commitment. Praise the Lord!

Remember Adam's soul became alive when the **Holy Spirit, Ruach Hakodesh** breathed <u>life</u> into him. (Old Testament) When we receive Jesus as our Lord and Savior **"our old life"** is exchanged for a **"new life"**. We become a new creature in Christ Jesus **2 Corinthians 5:17** (New Testament).

<u>John 6:63</u> says this, *It is the Spirit that quickeneth (or makes alive), the flesh profits nothing. In other words it is not a work of the flesh. The words that I speak unto you, they are Spirit and they are Life.*

 These are the attributes of the Holy Spirit's personality.

1. He is Truth and knows and searches everything in order to reveal Truth to us

<u>1 Corinthians 2: 9-11</u> – *But as it is written: "Eye has not seen, nor ear heard, nor have entered into the heart of man the things which God has prepared for those who love Him." **10** But God has revealed them to us through His Spirit. For the Spirit searches all things, yes, and the deep things of God. **11** For what man knows the things of a man except the spirit of the man which is in him? Even so no one knows the things of God except the Spirit of God.*

Anything that we want to know that is Truth about God or His Kingdom, the Holy Spirit will reveal it to us.

2. He can or will withdraw His Presence

<u>1 Samuel 16:14</u> *But the Spirit of the Lord departed from Saul, and a distressing spirit from the Lord troubled him*

<u>1 Samuel 18:12</u> – *And Saul was afraid of David because the Lord was with him, and He had departed from Saul.*

Psalm 51:11 *Do not cast me away from Your presence, And do not take Your Holy Spirit from me. 12 Restore to me the joy of Your salvation, And uphold me by Your generous Spirit.*

Judges 16: 20, 28 *And Delilah said, "The Philistines are upon you, Samson!" So he awoke from his sleep, and said, "I will go out as before, at other times, and shake myself free!"* **But he did not know that the Lord had departed from him.** *28 Then Samson called to the Lord, saying, "O Lord God, remember me, I pray! Strengthen me, I pray, just this once, O God that I may with one blow take vengeance on the Philistines for my two eyes!"* **The Holy Spirit is the might/power/strength of the Godhead and it was He who empowered Samson with his strength.**

3. He does not like to be grieved (grieved in this sense means to distress, cause grief or make sad)

Ephesians 4:30- *And do not grieve the Holy Spirit of God, by whom you were sealed for the day of redemption. 31 Let all bitterness, wrath, anger, clamor, and evil speaking be put away from you, with all malice.* **These are some of the things that grieve the Holy Spirit.**

Isaiah 63:10- *For He said, "Surely they are My people,* <u>*Children who will not lie.*</u>*" So He became their Savior. 9 In all their affliction He was afflicted, And the Angel of His Presence saved them; In His love and in His pity He redeemed them; And He bore them and carried them all the days of old. 10* <u>**But they rebelled and grieved His Holy Spirit;**</u> *So He turned Himself against them as an enemy, And He fought against them.*

Acts 7:51- *Has My hand not made all these things?' 51 "You stiff-necked and uncircumcised in heart and ears! You always resist the Holy Spirit; as your fathers did, so do you.*

4. He does not like to be lied to or to be deceived

<u>Acts 5:3-</u> *But a certain man named Ananias, with Sapphira his wife, sold a possession. 2 And he kept back part of the proceeds, his wife also being aware of it, and brought a certain part and laid it at the apostles' feet. 3 But Peter said, "Ananias, <u>**why has Satan filled your heart to lie to the Holy Spirit**</u> and keep back part of the price of the land for yourself.*

5. He will not extend forgiveness if blasphemed

<u>**What does the bible say about Blasphemy**</u> -to speak irreverently of God or sacred things; to speak evil of God, to slander (defame His character, malign Him with malicious intent) or abuse God.

<u>Matthew 12:32-</u> *Anyone who speaks a word against the <u>Son of Man</u> (means a human being not Jesus the Christ) , it will be forgiven him; but whoever speaks against the Holy Spirit, it will not be forgiven him, either in this age or in the age to come.*

<u>Mark 3:28-29</u> - *"Assuredly, I say to you, all sins will be forgiven the sons of men, and whatever blasphemies they may utter; 29 but he who blasphemes against the Holy Spirit never has forgiveness, but is subject to eternal condemnation".*

<u>Luke 12:10</u> - *And anyone who speaks a word against the Son of Man, it will be forgiven him; but to him who blasphemes against the Holy Spirit, it will not be forgiven.*

Biblical example of accusations of blasphemy-

<u>Acts 6: 8-15-</u> *And Stephen, full of faith and power, did great wonders and signs among the people. 9 Then there arose some from what is called the Synagogue of the Freedmen (Cyrenians, Alexandrians, and those from Cilicia and Asia), disputing with Stephen. 10 And they were not able to resist the wisdom and the Spirit by which he spoke. 11 Then they secretly induced men to say, "We have heard him speak blasphemous words against Moses and God." 12 And they stirred up the people, the elders, and the*

scribes; and they came upon him, seized him, and brought him to the council.
13 They also set up false witnesses who said, "This man does not cease to
speak blasphemous words against this holy place and the law; 14 for we have
heard him say that this Jesus of Nazareth will destroy this place and change
the customs which Moses delivered to us." 15 And all who sat in the council,
looking steadfastly at him, saw his face as the face of an angel.

6. He will commission or appoint us for service:

Commission: In other words the Holy Spirit commits or entrusts a
person with supervisory power or authority; He gives an
authoritative order, charge or direction.

Acts 13:2-4- As they ministered to the Lord and fasted, (as they
functioned in their roles as public servants to worship and be
obedient) the Holy Spirit **said,** (let me clarify this word "said" which
is the Greek and Hebrew word <u>Epo</u> which is to *speak* or *say* (by word
or by writing). It also implies to answer, to bid, to bring word, to call,
grant or command. In other words <u>the Holy Spirit will answer us; bid</u>
<u>us to come; bring a word; command us; grant us authority for a</u>
<u>specific task or function.</u> This is what the Holy Spirit did when he
instructed the apostles to "separate to himself Barnabus and Saul for
the work to which they were being sent to carry out. *"3 Then, having*
fasted and prayed, and laid hands on them, they sent them away. 4 So, being
sent out by the Holy Spirit, *they went down to Seleucia, and from there*
they sailed to Cyprus.

John 1: 30-32 John said this of Jesus-
*After me comes **a Man** who is preferred before me, for He was before me.' 31*
I did not know Him; but that He should be revealed to Israel, therefore I came
baptizing with water." 32 And John bore witness, saying, "I saw the Spirit
*descending from heaven **like a dove, and He remained upon Him.** 33 I*
did not know Him, but He who sent me to baptize with water said to me,
*'Upon whom you see **the Spirit descending, and remaining on Him, this***
is He who baptizes with the Holy Spirit.

Jesus was empowered by the Holy Spirit as a MAN….The Holy Spirit remained with Jesus and working with him throughout his ministry.

Luke 4:1 *And Jesus* (as a MAN) *being **full of the Holy Ghost** returned from Jordan, and was **led by the Spirit** into the wilderness.* This was to test the flesh of Man; to reveal to Man that it is the Holy Spirit and the Word working together to defeat Satan.

Luke 4:14 And *Jesus returned in the power of the Spirit into Galilee and there went out a fame of him through all the region round about.*

Luke 4:18 Jesus was commissioned to:

1. Carry the anointing

2. Preach the gospel to the poor

3. Heal broken lives

4. Preach deliverance to the captives

5. Recover lost vision

6. Liberate the captives

7. Preach a timeless message

Luke 4:32 *And they were astonished at His doctrine: for His word was with power* (mastery, force, authority). God's validation that a "Man full of the Holy Spirit" could once again dominate the Devil and walk in DOMINION!

What does the work of the Holy Spirit in the believer's life look like?

John 14:16, 17 *And I will pray the Father, and He will give you another Helper, that He may abide with you forever — **the Holy Spirit is our helper in the Earth and Jesus is our Helper in Heaven** 17 the Spirit of Truth,* *whom the world cannot receive, because it neither sees Him nor knows Him; but you know Him, for He dwells with you and will be in you.*

The Holy Spirit helps in the following ways:

A **Helper** is one who **assists,** works alongside of someone, one who **supports** and bears one up to sustain and corroborates. **Our Helper agrees with the Father and Jesus about us** and is the one who alleviates and removes the burden, carries the weight or load on our behalf. **This kind of help is for the Natural man.**

Greek word for "helper" is parakletos defining the role of Intercessor, Advocate, Counselor and Comforter. **This kind of help is for the Spiritual man.**

Earthly Intercessor One who prays or mediates on one's behalf. **Romans 8:26-28**-*Likewise the Spirit also **helps** in our weaknesses. (feeble in mind or body, weak) For we do not know what we should pray for as we ought, but the **Spirit Himself makes intercession** for us with groaning (to murmur, to sigh or pray inaudibly) which cannot be uttered. 27 Now He who **searches** (investigates the thoughts and feelings) the hearts **knows** (perceives and understands the inclinations or purpose, whether carnally or spiritually) what the mind of the Spirit is, because He makes intercession for the saints according to the will of God. 28 And we know that all things work together for good to those who love God, to those who are the called according to His purpose.*

Earthly Advocate One who defends.

Isaiah 59:19 *So shall they fear the name of the Lord from the west, And His Glory from the rising of the sun; When the enemy comes in like a flood, **The Spirit of the Lord** will lift up a standard against him. **This scripture is often referred to by Christians who are struggling which is okay in prayer application. But this scripture will literally be fulfilled when the enemies of Israel invade Israel in an effort to destroy the Jewish***

nation and to stop Christ from setting up His kingdom at His second coming.

<u>1 John 2:1</u> *My little children, these things I write to you, so that you may not sin. And if anyone sins, we have an **Advocate with the Father, Jesus Christ the righteous**.*

<u>Mark 13:11</u> *But when they arrest you and deliver you up, do not worry beforehand, or premeditate what you will speak. But whatever is given you in that hour, speak that; for it is not you who speak, but the Holy Spirit.*

The Complete Jewish Bible renders this version: 11 *Now when they arrest you and bring you to trial, don't worry beforehand about what to say. Rather, say whatever is given you when the time comes; for it will not be just you speaking, but the* **Ruach HaKodesh**.

Earthly Counselor *(Ruach HaKodesh)* One who advises.

<u>John 16:13</u>-*However, when He, the Spirit of Truth, has come,* **He will guide you** *into all truth; for He will not speak on His own authority, but* **whatever He hears He will speak; and He will tell you things to come.** *John 14:26 - But the Helper, the Holy Spirit, whom the Father will send in My name, He will teach you all things, and* **bring to your remembrance all things that I said to you.**

Earthly Comforter One who brings consolation and or edification. <u>Acts 9:31</u> *Then the churches throughout all Judea, Galilee, and Samaria had peace and were edified. And walking in the fear of the Lord and in the comfort of the Holy Spirit, they were multiplied.*

Examples of The Holy Spirit as our Helper/Teacher

<u>Acts 1:13</u> Philip named among the other disciples in the upper room.
<u>Acts 2:4</u> Philip was filled with the Holy Spirit and spoke in tongues.
<u>Acts 8:5,6</u> *Then Philip went down to the city of Samaria and preached Christ to them. 6 And the multitudes with one accord heeded the things spoken by Philip, hearing and seeing the miracles which he did.*

Acts 8:26-40 *Now an angel of the Lord spoke to Philip, saying, "Arise and go toward the south along the road which goes down from Jerusalem to Gaza." This is desert. **27** So he arose and went. And behold, **a man of Ethiopia, a eunuch of great authority under Candace** the queen of the Ethiopians, who had charge of all her treasury, and had come to Jerusalem to worship, **28** was returning. And sitting in his chariot, he was reading Isaiah the prophet. **29 Then the Spirit said to Philip, "Go near and overtake this chariot." 30** So Philip ran to him, and heard him reading the prophet Isaiah, and said, "Do you understand what you are reading?" **31 And he said, "How can I, unless someone guides me?" And he asked Philip to come up and sit with him. 32** The place in the Scripture which he read was this: "He was led as a sheep to the slaughter; And as a lamb before its shearer is silent, so He opened not His mouth. **33** In His humiliation His justice was taken away, And who will declare His generation? For His life is taken from the earth." **34 So the eunuch answered Philip and said, "I ask you, of whom does the prophet say this, of himself or of some other man?"** 35 Then Philip opened his mouth, and beginning at this Scripture, preached Jesus to him. 36 Now as they went down the road, they came to some water. And the eunuch said, "See, here is water. What hinders me from being baptized?" **37 Then Philip said, "If you believe with all your heart, you may." And he answered and said, "I believe that Jesus Christ is the Son of God." 38 So he commanded the chariot to stand still. And both Philip and the eunuch went down into the water, and he baptized him. 39 Now when they came up out of the water, the Spirit of the Lord caught Philip away,** so that the eunuch saw him no more; and he went on his way rejoicing. **40** But **Philip was found at Azotus. And passing through he preached in all the cities till he came to Caesarea.***

The Holy Spirit Sanctifies us.

Romans 15:16 *that I might be a minister of Jesus Christ to the Gentiles, ministering the gospel of God that the offering of the Gentiles might be acceptable, sanctified by the Holy Spirit.*

Sanctify = set apart as or declare holy; consecrate.

consecrate = make or declare Holy
dedicate formally to a religious or divine purpose

27

The Holy Spirit Convicts us or Reproves us.

John 16: 8 *And when He has come, He will convict the world of sin,* (makes us aware of our sin to give us an opportunity to turn away from the sin and repent) *and of righteousness,* (our righteousness is useless, filthy rags, but will be made righteous if atoned for) *and of judgment* (believers escape the judgement once atoned for. It is the unbeliever that will be judged).

The Holy Spirit Empowers us.

Acts 1:8: *But you will receive power when the **Ruach HaKodesh** comes upon you; you will be my witnesses both in Yerushalayim (Jerusalem) and in all Y'hudah (Judah) and Shomron, (Samaria) indeed to the ends of the earth!*

Lesson 3

The New Birth and Water Baptism

There are two manifestations of the Holy Spirit in relation to the believer. One has to do with the New Birth (the born again experience) and the other with the Baptism of the Holy Spirit (to be empowered by the Holy Spirit). Let me say right here, that there is a difference between **Water Baptism** and the **Holy Spirit Baptism.** In this lesson our goal is to weave together His function of sanctification, conviction and empowerment as they relate to us living a life totally controlled by Him and operating in His gifts and fruits.

The Holy Spirit is the Author of the New Birth

John 3:1-8 *There was a man of the Pharisees named Nicodemus, a ruler of the Jews. 2 This man came to Jesus by night and said to Him, "Rabbi, we know that You are a Teacher come from God; for no one can do these signs that You do unless God is with him." 3 Jesus answered and said to him, "Most assuredly, I say to you, **unless one is born again, he cannot see the kingdom of God."** 4 Nicodemus said to Him, "How can a man be born when he is old? Can he enter a second time into his mother's womb and be born?" 5 Jesus answered, **"Most assuredly, I say to you, unless one is born of water and the Spirit, he cannot enter the kingdom of God.** 6 That which is born of the flesh is flesh, and that **which is born of the Spirit is Spirit.** 7 Do not marvel that I said to you, 'You must be born again.' 8 The wind blows where it wishes, and you hear the sound of it, but cannot tell where it comes from and where it goes. **So is everyone who is born of the Spirit."***

Romans 10:10 *For with the heart one believes unto righteousness, and with the mouth confession is made unto salvation.*

Galatians 4:4 *But when the fullness of the time had come, God sent forth His Son, __born of a woman, born under the law__, 5 to redeem those who were under the law, that we might receive the adoption as sons (this is what sonship looks like). 6 And because you are sons, God has sent forth __the Spirit, Ruach HaKodesh__ of His Son into your hearts, crying out, "Abba, Father!" (The Holy Spirit will open the door for us to become engrafted as heirs) 7 Therefore you are no longer a slave but a son, and if a son, then an heir of God through Christ.*

These scriptures indicate to us that Jesus, who put on humanity, is our example of a "born again" life. He had always existed in Deity in the beginning. Because of the fall of mankind He needed to make a way for man to be "born again" by His Spirit. Jesus was our role model to show us how to live a born again life.

Romans 8:14-16 *For as many as are led by the Spirit of God, these are sons of God. 15 For you did not receive the spirit of bondage again to fear, but you received the Spirit of adoption by whom we cry out, "Abba, Father." 16 The Spirit Himself bears witness with our spirit that we are children of God,* **(Again, the Holy Spirit giving witness of his work of "new birth" in those who call upon Jesus as Savior).**

Romans 8 clearly lays out for the believer, the transformation of his "old life and old nature to his new life and new nature", giving evidence that it is the **work of the Holy Spirit, *Ruach HaKodesh*** that enables us as believers to have victory over sin and the sin nature. Also to live as sons and heirs of the kingdom. This is what it looks like to *Live Life in the Kingdom.*

1 John 5:4 *For whatever is born of God overcomes the world. And this is the* __victory that has overcome the world__*--our faith. 5 Who is he who overcomes the world, but he who believes that Jesus is the Son of God? (In other words when we receive Jesus as Savior we are empowered by the* **Holy Spirit, Ruach HaKodesh** *to live a life of victory in this "new birth experience".) 6 This is He who came by* __water and blood, Jesus Christ;__

not only by water, but by water and blood. *And it is the Spirit who bears witness, because the Spirit is Truth. 7 For there are three that bear witness in heaven: the Father, the Word, and the Holy Spirit; and* **these three are one.** *(The Holy Trinity) 8 And there are* **three that bear witness** *on earth: the Spirit, the water, and the blood; and* **these three agree as one***. Remember Nicodemus was told he had to be born again, born of the Spirit and water. Nicodemus was already a man with a flesh and blood body unlike Jesus, which is why Jesus had to take on the form of flesh in order to redeem mankind from a fallen state.*

Let's look to the New Testament at an Old Testament allegory (symbolic narrative) which alludes to the "new birth experience", as well as a "new covenant".

<u>Galatians 4:22-31</u> *For it is written that Abraham had two sons: the* **one by a bondwoman, the other by a freewoman. 23 But he who was of the bondwoman was born according to the flesh, and he of the freewoman through promise, 24 which things are symbolic.** *For these are the two covenants: the* **one** *from Mount Sinai which* **gives birth to bondage, which is Hagar,** *25 for this Hagar is Mount Sinai in Arabia, and corresponds to Jerusalem which now is, and is in bondage with her children,* **26 but the Jerusalem above is free, which is the mother of us all.** *27 For it is written: "Rejoice, O barren, You who do not bear! Break forth and shout, You who are not in labor! For the desolate has many more children than she who has a husband."* **28 Now we, brethren, as Isaac was, are children of promise. 29** *But, as he who was born according to the flesh* **then persecuted him who was born according to the Spirit, even so it is now.**

It was the **Holy Spirit, Ruach HaKodesh** that brought forth new life in Mary's womb, it was the **Holy Spirit, Ruach HaKodesh** that brought new life to Jesus in the grave after Calvary and it was the **Holy Spirit, Ruach HaKodesh** that brought new life to the "deadness of Sarah's womb ". The **Holy Spirit, Ruach HaKodesh** brings new life through the born again experience in the believer's life!

Evidence of the New Birth:

A moral and spiritual change takes place in the life of the believer.

A change of heart, motives, will, conduct, desires and lifestyles.

A change of masters (God vs Satan).

A change in status from slave to sonship.

A manifestation of spiritual gifts and the fruits of His spirit.

The Baptism of the Holy Spirit and Water Baptism

<u>Acts 1:4, 5</u> *And being assembled together with them, He commanded them not to depart from Jerusalem, but to wait for the Promise of the Father, "which," He said, "you have heard from Me; 5 for John truly* **baptized with water, but you shall be baptized with the Holy Spirit** *not many days from now."*

<u>Matthew 3: 5, 6,</u> *Then Jerusalem, all Judea, and all the region around the Jordan went out to him 6 and* **were baptized by him in the Jordan, confessing their sins. Then Jesus came from Galilee to John at the Jordan to be baptized by him.** *14 And John tried to prevent Him, saying, "I need to be baptized by You, and are You coming to me?" 15 But Jesus answered and said to him, "Permit it to be so now, for thus it is fitting for us to fulfill all righteousness." Then he allowed Him.* **16 When He had been baptized, Jesus came up immediately from the water;** *and behold, the heavens were opened to Him, and He saw the Spirit of God descending like a dove and alighting upon Him.*

<u>In Acts 2:14-39</u> *Peter who had just experienced the* **baptism of the Holy Spirit** *stood before the men of Judea and Israel who were devout Jews and some who were proselytes* **(a person who changes from one opinion or religious belief to another, a convert)** *to preach about Jesus's death, burial and resurrection and the promise of the Holy Spirit's outpouring.*

Let's pick up in verse 36 "Therefore let all the house of Israel know assuredly that God has made this Jesus, whom you crucified, both Lord and Christ." **37** Now when they heard this, they were cut to the heart, and said to Peter and the rest of the apostles, "Men and brethren, what shall we do?" **38** Then Peter said to them, *"Repent, and let every one of you be baptized in the name of Jesus Christ for the remission of sins; and you shall receive the gift of the Holy Spirit.* **39** For the promise is to you and to your children, and to all who are afar off, as many as the Lord our God will call.

In other words **all who repented** were **water baptized in Jesus name** and were in position to receive the gift of the Holy Spirit **(the baptism of the Holy Spirit).** The outward manifestation of this baptism would be to have the ability to speak in tongues, as Peter and those who were in the Upper Room had just received.

<u>Acts 8: 5-24</u> *Then Philip went down to the city of Samaria and preached Christ to them. 6 And the multitudes with one accord heeded the things spoken by Philip, hearing and seeing the miracles which he did. 7 For unclean spirits, crying with a loud voice, came out of many who were possessed; and many who were paralyzed and lame were healed. 8 And there was great joy in that city. 9 But there was a certain man called Simon, **who previously practiced sorcery in the city and astonished the people of Samaria, claiming that he was someone great,** 10 to whom they all gave heed, from the least to the greatest, saying, "This man is the great power of God." 11 And they heeded him because he had astonished them with his sorceries for a long time. 12 **But when they believed Philip as he preached the things concerning the kingdom of God and the name of Jesus Christ, both men and women were baptized. 13 Then Simon himself also believed; and when he was baptized he continued with Philip, and was amazed, seeing the miracles and signs which were done.** 14* Now when the apostles who were at Jerusalem heard that Samaria had received the word of God, they sent Peter and John to them, **15** who, when they had come down, prayed for them that they might receive the Holy Spirit. **16** For as yet He had fallen upon none of them. *They had only been baptized in the name of the Lord Jesus. 17 Then they laid hands on them, and they received the Holy Spirit. 18 And when Simon saw that through the laying on of the apostles'* *hands the Holy Spirit was given, he offered them money, 19 saying, "Give me this power also, that anyone on whom I lay hands may receive the Holy Spirit."* **20** But Peter said to him, "Your money perish with you, because **you thought that the gift of God could be purchased with money!** 21 *You have neither part nor portion in this matter, for your heart is not right in the sight of God.* **(No true conversion took place in his heart). We must take great care not to merchandise the gifts of The Holy Spirit. 22 Repent therefore of this your wickedness,** *and pray God if perhaps the thought of your heart may be forgiven you. 23 For I see that you are poisoned by bitterness and bound by iniquity."* **24** *Then Simon answered and said,* **"Pray to the Lord for me,** *that none of the things which you have spoken may come upon me."* This lets me believe that because Simon did not pray for himself but asked Peter and John to pray that no conversion took place. There was no heart repentance, no remorse for his actions.

Lesson 4

New Birth New Life

In review, we discussed the two manifestations of the Holy Spirit in relation to the believer. The **New Birth which is the born again experience signified by Water Baptism and the Baptism of the Holy Spirit which is to be empowered for ministry signified by an outward manifestation of speaking in tongues**.

Based upon the Word we come to the conclusion that both Water Baptism and Baptism of the Holy Spirit are two different experiences but also should be experienced by every believer just as Jesus demonstrated before He was released for ministry. **Jesus was Water Baptized and Baptized with the Holy Spirit as a Man in a flesh and blood body.**

Luke 3:21, *when all the people were baptized, it came to pass that Jesus also was baptized; and while He prayed, the heaven was opened.* **22** *And the Holy Spirit descended in bodily form like a dove upon Him, and a voice came from heaven which said, "You are My beloved Son; in You I am well pleased."*

John 1:29-34 *the next day John saw Jesus coming toward him, and said, "Behold! The Lamb of God who takes away the sin of the world!* **30** *This is He of whom I said, 'After me comes a Man who is preferred before me, for He was before me.'* **31** *I did not know Him; but that He should be revealed to Israel, therefore I came baptizing with water."* **32** *And John bore witness, saying, "I saw the Spirit descending from heaven like a dove, and He remained upon Him.* **33** *I did not know Him, but He who sent me to baptize with water said to me, 'Upon whom you see the Spirit descending, and remaining on Him, this is He who baptizes with the Holy Spirit.'* **34** *And I have seen and testified that this is the Son of God."*

Acts 10:38 *how God **anointed Jesus of Nazareth with the Holy Spirit and with power,** who went about doing good and healing all who were oppressed by the devil, for God was with Him.*

For greater clarity I will be using the New King James, The Complete Jewish Bible and the Common English Bible as we get ready to discuss the sanctification process which the Holy Spirit uses to prepare us for ministry and a lifestyle that is controlled by Him, evidenced by His gifts and His fruit.

Question: What does sanctification mean to the believer and what is portrayed to the unbeliever?

Sanctification is not wearing special clothing, whether that be long dresses, short dresses, pants or pantsuits, or suits and ties; it is not the forbidding of make-up, jewelry or foods to consume or not to consume, holidays to observe or not to observe which were all supposed to give believers a sense of spirituality and depict a morally cleansed lifestyle; all pointing to an outward appearance of salvation or religious standing that came by the "doctrines of man.

Paul addressed legalism when he wrote to the Colossian church. Chapter 2: 8, 16-23 *Be careful not to let anyone rob you (of this faith) through a shallow and misleading philosophy. Such a person follows human traditions and the world's way of doing things rather than following Christ. 16 Therefore, let no one judge you because of what you eat or drink or about the observance of annual holy days, New Moon Festivals, or weekly worship days. 20 If you have died with Christ to the world's way of doing things, why do you let others tell you how to live? It's as though you were still under the world's influence. 21 People will tell you, "Don't handle this! Don't taste or touch that!" 22 All of these things deal with objects that are only used up anyway. 23 These things look like wisdom with their self-imposed worship, false humility, and harsh treatment of the body, but they have no value for holding back the constant desires of your corrupt nature.* For the Old Testament saints, the Holy Spirit only came upon them for specific purposes. Sanctification in the Old Testament was exhibited by circumcision and/or the "outward washing of clothing"; keeping oneself from intimate sexual contact for a period of time and sometimes included fasting.

Exodus 19: 4-11 (outward) says-*The children of Israel had just been delivered from bondage and Pharaoh's dominion. The LORD called to Moses from the mountain, "This is what you should say to Jacob's household and declare to the Israelites:*

*4 You saw what I did to the Egyptians, and how I lifted you up on eagles' wings and brought you to me. 5 So now, if you faithfully obey me and stay true to my covenant, you will be my most precious possession out of all the peoples, since the whole earth belongs to me. 6 **You will be a kingdom of priests for me and a holy nation.** These are the words you should say to the Israelites." 9 Then the LORD said to Moses, **"I'm about to come to you in a thick cloud in order that the people will hear me talking with you so that they will always trust you."** Moses told the LORD what the people said, **10 and the LORD said to Moses: "Go to the people and take today and tomorrow to make them holy. Have them wash their clothes.** 11 Be ready for the third day, because on the third day the LORD will come down on Mount Sinai for all the people to see.*

Moses had to prepare the people for a Divine encounter with the Lord. They had to be cleansed from the "old life of slavery and bondage from Egyptian living. We must prepare ourselves to have Divine encounters with the Lord. First, we must cleanses our minds from thoughts that hold us in bondage to our old nature and old past. Then we must walk in the newness of our redeemed lives!

1 Chronicles 15:14 The priests and the Levites sanctified (cleansed) themselves to bring up the ark of the Lord.

Jeremiah 1:5 Jeremiah was sanctified (set apart) in his mother's womb to be a prophet to the Nations. A Prophet was a Seer who spoke prophetically and had keen discernment regarding natural and spiritual things.

In the New Testament and in our dispensation, sanctification is demonstrated by an "inward work of the Holy Spirit."

Romans 15:16 (inward) says that I might be a minister of Jesus Christ to the Gentiles, ministering the gospel of God, that the offering of the Gentiles might be acceptable and **sanctified by the Holy Spirit.**

Sanctification is more than just having your character morally changed when you are brought to the Truth of God's Word. The Holy Spirit will *work in your nature* **to** bring you under His influence by revealing the Kingdoms principles of grace and regeneration. **In other words, it is "working out you own souls salvation" which started the day you accepted Jesus as Savior. The process of sanctification is solidified when you make Jesus Lord and Master. You become His bondservant. A bondservant relinquishes his rights to make decisions for himself. He is a true servant to his Master.**

Romans 6:12-14 *Therefore, do not let sin rule in your mortal bodies, so that it makes you obey its desires; 13 and do not offer any part of yourselves to sin as an instrument for wickedness. On the contrary, offer yourselves to God as people alive from the dead, and your various parts to God as instruments for righteousness. 14 For sin will not have authority over you; because you are not under legalism but under grace.*

1 Corinthians 6: 9-12

Paul poses a question to a group of carnal believers who had been living according to their own natural desires. *9 **Do you not know that the unrighteous will not inherit the kingdom of God?** Do not be deceived. Neither fornicators, nor idolaters, nor adulterers, nor homosexuals, nor sodomites, 10 nor thieves, nor covetous, nor drunkards, nor revilers, nor* *extortionist will inherit the kingdom of God. 11 And such were some of you.* **But you were washed, but you were sanctified, but you were justified in the name of the Lord Jesus and by the Spirit of our God.** *12 All things are lawful for me, but all things are not helpful. All things are lawful for me, but I will not be brought under the power of any.*

Do you see what Paul said.......he said he will not let anything have dominion over him or his body. We have the POWER to stay FREE!

<u>John 17:16-19</u> Jesus' is speaking to the Father and says- *They are not of the world, just as I am not of the world. 17 Sanctify them by Your truth. Your word is truth.* **(The Holy Spirit is the Spirit of Truth)** *18 As You sent Me into the world, I also have sent them into the world. 19 And for their sakes I sanctify Myself, that they also may be sanctified by the truth.* **The Word separates us from the world and from our old nature.**

<u>John 16:7-11</u> *Nevertheless I tell you the truth. It is to your advantage that I go away; for if I do not go away, the Helper will not come to you; but if I depart, I will send Him to you. 8 And when He has come, He will convict the world of sin, and of righteousness, and of judgment: 9 of sin, because they do not believe in Me; 10 of righteousness, because I go to My Father and you see Me no more; 11 of judgment, because the ruler of this world is judged.*

The more the process of sanctification takes root in your soul, the more and more you become sensitive to sin and deepen your relationship with Christ. Sin begins to bother you. You begin to "hate" what God "hates". The warfare of your mind, your will and your emotions will intensify......there will be a constant tugging between the "old nature or old man and the new nature and the new man.

Saul whose name was changed to Paul is a perfect example of Sanctification by the Holy Spirit.

<u>Acts 9: 1-22;</u> *- Then Saul, still breathing threats and murder against the disciples of the Lord, went to the high priest 2 and asked letters from him to*

the synagogues of Damascus, so that if he found any who were of the Way, whether men or women, he might bring them bound to Jerusalem. *3* As he journeyed he came near Damascus, and suddenly a light shone around him from heaven. *4* Then he fell to the ground, and heard a voice saying to him, "Saul, Saul, why are you persecuting Me?" *5* And he said, "Who are You, Lord?" Then the Lord said, "I am Jesus, whom you are persecuting. It is hard for you to kick against the goads." *6* So he, trembling and astonished, said, "Lord, what do You want me to do?" Then the Lord said to him, "Arise and go into the city, and you will be told what you must do." *7* And the men who journeyed with him stood speechless, hearing a voice but seeing no one. *8* Then Saul arose from the ground, and when his eyes were opened he saw no one. But they led him by the hand and brought him into Damascus. *9* **And he was three days without sight, and neither ate nor drank. 10** Now there was a certain disciple at Damascus named Ananias; and to him the Lord said in a vision, "Ananias." And he said, "Here I am, Lord." *11* So the Lord said to him, "Arise and go to the street called Straight, and inquire at the house of Judas for one called Saul of Tarsus, for behold, he is praying. *12* And in a vision he has seen a man named Ananias coming in and putting his hand on him, so that he might receive his sight." *13* Then Ananias answered, "Lord, I have heard from many about this man, how much harm he has done to Your saints in Jerusalem. *14* And here he has authority from the chief priests to bind all who call on Your name." *15* But the Lord said to him, "**Go, for he is a chosen vessel of Mine to bear My name before Gentiles, kings, and the children of Israel. 16 For I will show him how many things he must suffer for My name's sake.**" *17* And Ananias went his way and entered the house; and laying his hands on him he said, "Brother Saul, the Lord Jesus, who appeared to you on the road as you came, has sent me that you may receive your sight and **be filled with the Holy Spirit.**" **18 Immediately there fell from his eyes something like scales, and he received his sight at once; and he arose and was baptized.***19* So when he had received food, he was strengthened. Then Saul spent some days with the disciples at Damascus. *20* Immediately he preached the Christ in the synagogues, that He is the Son of God. *21* Then all who heard were amazed, *and said, "Is this not he who destroyed those who called on this name in Jerusalem, and has come here for that purpose, so that he might bring them bound to the chief priests?"* **22** But **Saul increased all the more in strength**, *and confounded the Jews who dwelt in Damascus, proving that this Jesus is the Christ.*

This is the **Power of the Word** transforming a life. You cannot encounter the Lord and stay the same. If it is a true encounter then there will be a transformation.

Romans 7:14-25 - Personal Reading

Philippians 3: 7-14 -Personal Reading

Romans 8 clearly lays out for the believer, the transformation of his "old life and old nature to his new life and new nature", giving evidence that it is the **work of the Holy Spirit, Ruach HaKodesh** that enables us as believers to have victory over sin and the sin nature. Also to live as sons and heirs of the kingdom. We will not attain to "perfection in sanctification" but we will become more reverent toward God and His Kingdom, we will become more humble and less self-righteous.

Lesson 5

Sanctified

Last lesson discussed the **sanctification process** which the Holy Spirit uses to prepare us for ministry, as well as, to live a lifestyle that is controlled by Him, which would be evidenced by His gifts and His fruit.

The Old Testament saints experienced the Holy Spirit coming upon them for specific purposes but now we experience an "inward work of the Holy Spirit to be God's children, God's ministers and His ambassadors.

We looked at Romans 15:16 in which Paul said that He might be a minister of Jesus Christ to the Gentiles, ministering the gospel of God, that the offering of the Gentiles might be acceptable and **sanctified by the Holy Spirit. In other words that non-believers would be presented with the Gospel of Christ and that they would have the opportunity to receive Him and be set apart by the Holy Spirit.**

Please understand that sanctification is more than just having your character morally changed when you are confronted with the Truth of God's Word. The Holy Spirit will **work in your nature** to bring you under His influence by revealing Kingdom principles and show you how to "**work out you own souls salvation**" which began the day you accepted Jesus as Savior.

In Romans 6 Paul is not only giving us instructions on how not to grieve the Presence of the Holy Spirt, but also to be a prepared vessel that can be used for God's kingdom work. He tells us:

1. Not to let sin rule in our mortal bodies whereby we would obey and or yield to its desires; passions and lust.

2. Not to become an instrument; tool, or weapon in Satan's hand for wickedness or sin.

3. He admonishes us to become an instrument or tool in God's hand for righteous living.

4. We are not to allow sin to have permission to govern or operate in our lives under any circumstances.

Let's revisit Romans 8

Verse 5-9 (Complete Jewish Bible) says this - *For those who identify with their old nature set their minds on the things of the old nature, but those who identify with the Spirit set their minds on the things of the Spirit. 6 Having one's mind controlled by the old nature is death, but having one's mind controlled by the Spirit is life and shalom. 7 For the mind controlled by the old nature is hostile to God, because it does not submit itself to God's Torah (law) indeed, it cannot. 8 Thus, those who identify with their old nature cannot please God. 9 But you, you do not identify with your old nature but with the Spirit - provided the Spirit of God is living inside you, for anyone who doesn't have the Spirit of the Messiah doesn't belong to him.*

I believe this is key in order for believers to live transformational lives. Demonstrating daily that the "old life and old nature have been put to death so that the new life and new nature", give evidence that through the **work of the Holy Spirit, Ruach HaKodesh** we will be empowered to become the manifestation of the "sons of God that the whole world is waiting to see as spoken of in verse 19. The world wants to see **"power, signs and wonders "**in the lives of believers. The Holy Spirit releases the gifts of the spirit in us to demonstrate that power and those wonders of God's kingdom as a witness to the unbeliever.

Paul's encounter with the Lord **(Acts 9)** was an example of what a "spirit filled life" and "spirit controlled life" looks like after being born again; living a sinful life versus living a life dedicated to the

Lord's purposes. Paul's life demonstrated the power, the signs and the wonders through the manifestation of spiritual gifts, throughout the book of Acts.

Over the next few lessons we are going to talk about how to live lives that are Spirit led and Spirit controlled and address the following questions:

1. How do I develop my spirit to obey the Holy Spirit?

2. What does it mean to walk in the Spirit?

3. How does the Holy Spirit lead us?

4. What does the anointing look like?

5. Do I need to be continually be filled with the Spirit?

Question 1. How do I develop my spirit to obey the Holy Spirit?

Answer: Become **God-inside minded** and acknowledge that the Greater One is living on the inside of you.

1 John 4: 4-6, 13, *You, children, are from God and have overcome the false prophets, because he who is in you is greater than he who is in the world. 5 They are from the world; therefore, they speak from the world's viewpoint; and the world listens to them. 6 We are from God. Whoever knows God listens to us; whoever is not from God doesn't listen to us. **This is how we distinguish the Spirit of truth from the spirit of error.** 13 Here is how we know that we remain united with him and He with us: **He has given to us from his own Spirit. God's powerhouse is within us!***

Galatians 2:19-20 *For I through the law died to the law that I might live to God. 20 I have been crucified with Christ; it is no longer I who live, but Christ lives in me; and the life which I now live in the flesh I live by faith in the Son of God, who loved me and gave Himself for me.*

45

Romans 12: 1, 2 (Complete Jewish Bible) *I exhort you, therefore, brothers, in view of God's mercies, to offer yourselves as a sacrifice, living and set apart for God. This will please him; it is the logical "Temple worship" for you. 2 In other words, do not let yourselves be conformed to the standards of the 'olam hazeh (Hebrew word meaning "world"). Instead,* **keep letting yourselves be transformed by the renewing of your minds; so that you will know what God wants and will agree that what he wants is good, satisfying and able to succeed.**

Reflection: **Genesis 22:1, 2 Abraham was told to offer up Isaac, the son of his flesh and blood as a sacrifice to God.**

Question: **What would be required of you? What is your Isaac?**

Isaiah 53: 10 *Yet it pleased the Lord to bruise Him; He has put Him to grief. When You make His soul an offering for sin, He shall see His seed, He shall prolong His days, And the pleasure of the Lord shall prosper in His hand.*

Ephesians 3:16-19 (cjb) *I pray that from the treasures of his glory he will* **empower you with inner strength by his Spirit**, *17 so that the Messiah may live in your hearts through your* **trusting**. *Also I pray that you will be* **rooted and founded in love, 18** *so that you, with all God's people,* **will be given strength to grasp the breadth, length, height and depth of the Messiah's love, 19** *yes, to know it, even though it is beyond all knowing,* **so that you will be filled with all the fullness of God.**

In other words, we must be fully convinced that it is God who strengthens our inner man with Himself. He fuses what is weak in us to Himself who is Strong. By trusting in Christ's finished work on our behalf we then become rooted and grounded and secure in His love, making it possible for Him to accomplish more than we can ask, think or imagine because it is His power that is being released through us. That is why Paul said "in **Hebrews 13: 20, 21** *Now may the God of peace who brought up our Lord Jesus from the dead, that great Shepherd of the sheep, through the blood of the everlasting covenant, 21 make you complete* *in every good work to do His will, working in you what is well pleasing in His sight, through Jesus Christ, to whom be glory forever and ever.*

<u>**Feed your Spirit on the following scriptures:**</u>

<u>**Philippians 1:6**</u> *being confident of this very thing that He who has begun a good work in you will complete it until the day of Jesus Christ;*

<u>**Colossians 3: 12-16**</u> *Therefore, as the elect of God, holy and beloved, put on tender mercies,* **kindness, humility, meekness, longsuffering;** *13 bearing with one another, and forgiving one another, if anyone has a complaint against another; even as Christ forgave you, so you also must do. 14 But above all these things put on* **love,** *which is the bond of perfection. 15 And let the peace of God rule in your hearts, to which also you were called in one body; and be thankful. 16 Let the word of Christ dwell in you richly in all wisdom, teaching and admonishing one another in psalms and hymns and spiritual songs, singing with grace in your hearts to the Lord.*

In other words, some of the **fruit of the Spirit** will begin to develop which is necessary for the effectiveness of the Holy Spirit's gifts to operate in our lives.

(Complete Jewish Bible) - *12 Therefore, as God's chosen people, holy and dearly loved, clothe yourselves with feelings of compassion and with kindness, humility, gentleness and patience. 13 Bear with one another; if anyone has a complaint against someone else, forgive him. Indeed, just as the Lord has forgiven you, so you must forgive. 14 Above all these, clothe yourselves with love, which binds everything together perfectly; 15 and let the Peace of God,* **the shalom of God** *which comes from the Messiah be your heart's decision-maker, for this is why you were called to be part of a single Body. And be thankful - 16 let the Word of the Messiah, in all its richness, live in you, as you teach and counsel each other in all wisdom, and as you sing psalms, hymns and spiritual songs with gratitude to God in your hearts.*

Reflection: Paul's transformed life had the following elements:
Read: Galatians 1:15-24

- Paul recognized that his sin was against God so he repented.
- Paul developed his "inner man or spirit" to obey and yield to the call on his life.
- Paul spent time in prayer, fasting and the study of the word.
- Paul learned how to hear the voice of the Holy Spirit.

Lesson 6

Walk in the Spirit

As we continue to think about Paul's life we recognize through his teaching in the New Testament that he reminds us that when we sin our sin is against God so God hopes we will repent. I say hope because God will not violate our "free will". We also see he admonishes us to develop our "inner man"; to train our spirit to obey and yield to the call placed upon our lives. Then finally, Paul spent time in prayer; fasting and the study of the word to learn how to hear the voice of the Holy Spirit.

Acts 9 Paul's encounter with the Lord is a model for the New Testament believer of what a "spirit filled life" and "spirit controlled life" looks like after being born again. Paul's life succinctly demonstrates the power, the signs and the wonders through the manifestation of spiritual gifts.

Reflection: The key to Paul's success is found in Romans 8. Read and meditate on this chapter.

The previous lesson we talked about and answered question 1. How do we develop our spirit to obey the Holy Spirit? In this lesson we are going to talk about question 2.

Question 2. What does it mean to walk in the Spirit?

In order to answer this question we must define what "walk "means relative to this text.

In the dictionary "walk" means to advance or travel on foot at a moderate speed or pace; move by advancing the feet alternatively or to proceed by steps.

In the Greek *"walk"* means to live a life or the conduct of one's life or lifestyle. It also means to follow; lead; grow.

In the Old Testament the Lord dealt with Abraham, *who would* become the Father of many nations and Moses, *who would* lead the children of Israel out of bondage regarding their walk and lifestyle.

Let's take a look:

Genesis 17:1 *When Avram was ninety-nine years old ADONAI appeared to Avram and said to him, "I am El Shaddai, God Almighty, "walk" in my Presence and be pure-hearted. 2 I will make my covenant between me and you and I will increase your numbers greatly."* **Abraham had the responsibility to live or model a lifestyle that was upright and pure-hearted before the people he would ultimate lead.**

Deuteronomy 10:12 Moses is speaking, *"And now, Israel, what does the Lord your God require of you, but to fear the Lord your God,* **to walk** *in all His ways and to love Him, to serve the Lord your God with all your heart and with all your soul. (nkjv)*

O now, Israel, all that ADONAI your God asks from you is to fear ADONAI your God, follow all His ways, love Him and serve ADONAI your God with all your heart and all your being. **Moses' responsibility was to train them to walk and live in accordance to the new law as well as be a role model before the people.** (cjb)

Deuteronomy 13:4 *You shall* **walk** *after the Lord your God and fear Him, and keep His commandments and obey His voice and you shall serve Him and hold fast to Him. (nkjv)*

You are to follow ADONAI your God, fear Him, obey his mitzvot (Commandments), listen to what He says, serve Him and cling to Him. (cjb)

Romans 8 says this:

1 Therefore, there is no longer any condemnation awaiting those who are in union with the Messiah Yeshua. **(There is no condemnation to those who do not walk according to the flesh or sin nature- nkjv)** *2 Why? Because the Torah of the Spirit, which produces this life in union with Messiah Yeshua, has set me free from the "Torah" of sin and death. 3 For what the Torah could not do by itself, because it lacked the power to make the old nature cooperate,* **(the old law was outside, it was an external work versus the new covenant which made it possible for us to be joined to the resurrected life of Jesus)** *God accomplished this by sending his own Son as a human being with a nature like our own sinful one, but without sin. God did this in order to deal with sin, and in so doing he executed the punishment against sin in human nature, 4 so that the just requirement of the Torah might be fulfilled in us who do not run our lives according to what our old nature wants but according to what the Spirit wants. 5 For those who identify with their old nature set their minds on the things of the old nature, but those who identify with the Spirit set their minds on the things of the Spirit. 6 Having one's mind controlled by the old nature is death, but having one's mind controlled by the Spirit is life and shalom. 7 For the mind controlled by the old nature is hostile to God, because it does not submit itself to God's Torah - indeed, it cannot. 8 Thus, those who identify with their old nature* **(Carnality)** *cannot please God.*

"Carnality is when you develop an attitude of unbelief" Dr. Bill Bright

Read: 2 Corinthians 3: 1-3 and Discuss as a group

9 But you, **you do not identify with your old nature but with the Spirit (provided the Spirit of God is living inside you)** *for anyone who doesn't have the Spirit of the Messiah doesn't belong to him. 10 However, if the Messiah is in you, then, on the one hand, the body is dead because of sin; but, on the other hand, the Spirit is giving life because God considers you righteous. 11 And if the Spirit of the One who raised Yeshua from the dead is living in you, then the One who raised the Messiah Yeshua from the dead will also give life to your mortal bodies through his Spirit living in you.*

12 So then, brothers, we don't owe a thing to our old nature that would require us to live according to our old nature. 13 For if you live according to your old nature, you will certainly die; but if, by the Spirit, you keep putting to death the practices of the body, you will live. 14 All who are led by God's Spirit are God's sons.

Reflection: Think about it like this: there is a throne, a control center that houses your intellect which sends signals through your mind, will and emotions. We all have this type of intellectual wiring. We will either allow self to rule or dominate from that place or the Holy Spirit and Jesus Christ the Word to rule from that throne.

<u>Galatians 5:16-21</u> *What I am saying is this: run or operate your lives by the Spirit. Then you will not do what your old nature wants. 17 For the old nature wants what is contrary to the Spirit, and the Spirit wants what is contrary to the old nature. These oppose each other, so that you find yourselves unable to carry out your good intentions. 18 But if you are led by the Spirit, then you are not in subjection to the system that results from perverting the Torah into legalism. 19 And it is perfectly evident what the old nature does. It expresses itself in sexual immorality, impurity and indecency; 20 involvement with the occult and with drugs; in feuding, fighting, becoming jealous and getting angry; in selfish ambition, factionalism, intrigue 21 and envy; in drunkenness, orgies and things like these. I warn you now as I have warned you before: those who do such things will have no share in the Kingdom of God!*

The late Dr. Bill Bright, Founder of Campus Crusade for Christ says this, "As you walk in the Spirit by faith, practice spiritual breathing. You will never again live in spiritual defeat. Spiritual breathing like physical breathing is a process of exhaling the impure and inhaling the pure, an exercise in faith that enables you to experience God's love and forgiveness and walk in the Spirit as a way of life."

Reverend A. B. Simpson, a Canadian preacher from the late 1800's and was known for his Evangelism and Pentecostal Effect wrote this about what it is to walk in the Spirit.

1. Maintain the habit of dependence upon the Holy Spirit for our entire life, spirit, soul and body.

2. Recognize that the Holy Spirit is present and abiding in us and He has come to our aid.

3. Trust the Holy Spirit and expect Him in the crisis and emergencies of your life. His very name Paraclete means He will be by our side when called upon. Expect Him to respond to us implicitly.

4. Consult the Holy Spirit. You will find the things that seem most easy will fail and disappoint us when we rely upon their apparent probability and the mere promise of outward circumstances. We shall also find where we commit our way to Him and acknowledge Him in all our ways that He will direct our paths and the things which seemed most difficult and impossible will become the easiest and the most successful.

5. Walking in the Spirit implies that we shall keep step with the Holy Spirit. Our obedience should be so prompt that we shall never find ourselves a step behind Him and following Him at a distance which we may find it hard to recover.

Dave Roberson (Oklahoma) Word of Prophecy

The Walk of the Spirit - 1999

Offer yourselves a living sacrifice through the eternal Spirit, says the Spirit of Grace. For I do desire even this day that you be not conformed to the world and its systems, but be transformed by the renewing of your mind that you may prove the good, acceptable and perfect will that I have separated you unto from the foundations of the earth. Oh that you might enter into the delicacies of the Spirit, that precious place of fellowship with Me, that dormitory of understanding, where I invite you into fellowship with Me, where things are seen through the eyes of the Spirit and your understanding is charged with My understanding. And I would say unto you that in this secret place of the Most High dwells the understanding and the power for your transformation. Therefore, pray and utilize the forces and the power of the Spirit within and pray, edifying yourself that you may enter in.......

My ADMONITION to you: Your feelings are unreliable, don't trust them.....WALK BY FAITH

Lesson 7

The Anointing

The previous lesson showed us "what it means to walk in the spirit, relative to the root word meaning follow; lead or to grow. We also know that Paul, who was born again after an encounter with the "light of the Word" in the person of Jesus was transformed by allowing the Holy Spirit to not only give revelation of the word but by renewing his mind. Paul made a change from living by "old traditional doctrine and legalism to living by the truth he received from the Holy Spirit.

Let me say this, when truth is spoken to our "new nature or new man" it will challenge the old paradigms, old doctrines, dogmas and religious mindsets. The Holy Spirit comes to transform us into the image, internally and externally to bear the resemblance of Christ in character and lifestyle.

Keep in mind that to walk in the spirit is **"a spirit filled and spirit controlled life"**. Walking in the spirit for a believer is to walk in step with the Holy Spirit through yielding continually to his voice and inward promptings or witness. **Part of our obedience is to listen for His instructions and then by faith act upon what we have heard**. When walking in the spirit we are trusting His guiding hand and committing all of our ways to His wisdom. <u>**Galatians 5:16**</u> says *"if we walk in the Spirit we shall not fulfill the lust of the flesh."* **Our life shall be transformed from a defensive warfare in which we are always attacking the devil to a God-inside minded position of awareness of our victory and power over the devil.** This kind of walk enables us to maintain the perfect harmony or balance between our inward life and our outward leanings.

<u>**Romans 8:14**</u> then becomes evidence of who we are....*for as many as are led of the Spirit of God, these are the sons of God.* Did you hear that,

these are they who are mature and no longer toddlers or adolescents; these are they who no longer want the "milk of the word" but are always hungry for the meaty things, the deep things of the Kingdom. Paul communicates this deep desire so eloquently when in **Philippians 3: 10 (cjb)** he says, *Yes, I gave it all up in order to know him, that is, to know the power of his resurrection and the fellowship of his sufferings as I am being conformed to his death,* **11** *so that somehow I might arrive at being resurrected from the dead.* **12** *It is not that I have already obtained it or already reached the goal no, I keep pursuing it in the hope of taking hold of that for which the Messiah Yeshua took hold of me.* ***In verse*** **13 *Paul tells us that he has not yet gotten hold of it; but one thing he does and that is to forget what was behind him and straining forward toward what lies ahead*, 14 *he keeps pursuing the goal in order to win the prize offered by God's upward calling in the Messiah Yeshua.*** *15 Therefore, as many of us are mature, let us keep paying attention to this; and if you are differently minded about anything, God will also reveal this to you. 16 Only let our conduct fit the level we have already reached. And he admonishes us to join in imitating him, and pay attention to those who live according to the pattern that is set before us.*
This kind of lifestyle is ready to "house "God's anointing.

Question 4. **What does the anointing in us look like?**

First of all, let's make sure we all have the same frame of reference as to what "is" the anointing.

It was interesting to me that the English definition and the Greek definition render the same meaning. To anoint is to rub, sprinkle, smear or apply ointment. To consecrate or make sacred by applying oil. To dedicate to the service of God.

Exodus 30: 22- 25 **(recipe for the biblical anointing oil)** Moreover the Lord spoke to Moses, saying: **23** "*Also take for yourself quality spices-five hundred shekels of liquid myrrh, half as much sweet-smelling cinnamon (two hundred and fifty shekels), two hundred and fifty shekels of sweet-smelling cane, 24 five hundred shekels of cassia, according to the shekel of the* *sanctuary, and a hin of olive oil. 25 And you shall make from these a holy anointing oil, an ointment compounded according to the art of the perfumer. It shall be a holy anointing oil.*

Now we will see an outward pouring of the Anointing

<u>Exodus 40:9-15</u> *And you shall take the anointing oil, and anoint the tabernacle and all that is in it; and you shall hallow it and all its utensils, and it shall be holy. 10 You shall anoint the altar of the burnt offering and all its utensils, and consecrate the altar. The altar shall be most holy. 11 And you shall anoint the laver and its base, and consecrate it. 12 Then you shall bring Aaron and his sons to the door of the tabernacle of meeting and wash them with water. 13 You shall put the holy garments on Aaron, and anoint him and consecrate him, that he may minister to Me as priest. 14 And you shall bring his sons and clothe them with tunics. 15 You shall anoint them, as you anointed their father, that they may minister to Me as priests; for their anointing shall surely be an everlasting priesthood throughout their generations."*

Examples of outward pouring of the anointing oil for purpose:
- Samuel anoints Saul as King over Israel- **1 Samuel 9:27, 1 Samuel 10:1**
- Samuel the Prophet anoints David as King – **1 Samuel 16:13**
- Elijah anointed Jehu King over Israel and Elisha as a prophet – **1 Kings 19:16**

<u>Isaiah 10: 24-27</u> **(cjb)**
*24 Therefore **ADONAI (sovereign) ELOHIM(triune)-Tzva'ot(Lord of Host)** says: "My people living in Tziyon,(Zion) don't be afraid of Ashur,(Assyrian enemy) even when he strikes you with a stick and raises his staff against you, the way it was in Egypt. 25 For in but a little while, my fury will end; and my anger will have destroyed them." 26 **ADONAI-Tzva'ot (sovereign lord of host)** will wield a whip against them, as he did when striking Midyan at the Rock of 'Orev; as his staff was over the sea, he will raise it, the way it was in Egypt. 27 On that day his burden will fall*

from your shoulders and his yoke from your neck; the yoke will be destroyed by your (prosperity- Greek word – Shemen (translates- fruitfulness, richness which is a quality of the oil of olives)

In other words, the day the enemy rises against you, the Sovereign Triune Lord of Host will be upon you to destroy the yoke that was a burden and put you in bondage because of the power of His anointing oil.

<u>Do you remember the harlot in Mark 14:3-5?</u> *And being in Bethany at the house of Simon the leper, as He sat at the table, a woman came having an alabaster flask of very costly oil of spikenard. Then she broke the flask and poured it on His head. 4 But there were some who were indignant among themselves, and said, "Why was this fragrant oil wasted? 5 For it might have been sold for more than three hundred denarii (year's wages) and given to the poor."* **And they criticized her sharply. 8. She has done what she could. She has come beforehand to anoint My body for burial.**

Here Jesus's body was anointed with oil to externally signify the power of the anointing to destroy the yoke and burden of death at Calvary. He would then have the power and authority to be risen from the dead and to set those who were held captive and those in bondage free. It is symbolic in that the yoke of death and the burden of sin was destroyed because of the anointing that was in Him and on Him.

Reflection ~ Read ~ Commit to Memory

<u>Acts 10:38</u> *how God anointed Jesus of Nazareth with the Holy Spirit and with power, who went about doing good and healing all who were oppressed by the devil, for God was with Him.*

<u>Luke 4: 1, 18</u> *Then Jesus, being filled with the Holy Spirit, returned from the Jordan and was led by the Spirit into the wilderness, 18 The Spirit of the Lord is upon Me, because He has anointed Me To preach the gospel to the poor; He has sent Me to heal the brokenhearted, To proclaim liberty to the*

captives And recovery of sight to the blind, To set at liberty those who are oppressed.

Romans 8:11 *But if the Spirit of Him who raised Jesus from the dead dwells in you, He who raised Christ from the dead will also give life to your mortal bodies through **His Spirit who dwells in you.***

Romans 8 reveals something else to us and that is – His anointing dwells within us if we are walking in the Spirit as sons/daughters.

<u>Anointing Within Us - 1 John 2:18-27</u>

18 Little children, it is the last hour; and as you have heard that the Antichrist is coming, even now many antichrists have come, by which we know that it is the last hour. 19 They went out from us, but they were not of us; for if they had been of us, they would have continued with us; but they went out that they might be made manifest, that none of them were of us. 20 But you have an anointing from the Holy One, and you know all things. 21 I have not written to you because you do not know the truth, but because you know it, and that no lie is of the truth. 22 Who is a liar but he who denies that Jesus is the Christ? He is antichrist who denies the Father and the Son. 23 Whoever denies the Son does not have the Father either; he who acknowledges the Son has the Father also. 24 Therefore let that abide in you which you heard from the beginning. If what you heard from the beginning abides in you, you also will abide in the Son and in the Father. 25 And this is the promise that He has promised us--eternal life. 26 These things I have written to you concerning those who try to deceive you. 27 But the anointing which you have received from Him abides in you, and you do not need that anyone teach you; but as the same anointing teaches you concerning all things, and is true, and is not a lie, and just as it has taught you, you will abide in Him.

<u>Anointing Upon Us - Acts 1:8</u> *"But you shall receive power when the Holy Spirit has come upon you; and you shall be witnesses to Me in Jerusalem, and in all Judea and Samaria, and to the end of the earth."*

Yielding to the Anointing:

Now we are ready to receive the ministry of the Holy Spirit

<u>Ephesians 4:17-30</u> *This I say, therefore, and testify in the Lord, that you should no longer walk as the rest of the Gentiles walk, in the futility of their mind, 18 having their understanding darkened, being alienated from the life of God, because of the ignorance that is in them, because of the blindness of their heart; 19 who, being past feeling, have given themselves over to lewdness, to work all uncleanness with greediness. 20 But you have not so learned Christ, 21 if indeed you have heard Him and have been taught by Him, as the truth is in Jesus: 22 that you put off, concerning your former conduct, the old man which grows corrupt according to the deceitful lusts, 23 and be renewed in the spirit of your mind, 24 and that you put on the new man which was created according to God, in true righteousness and holiness. 25 Therefore, putting away lying, "Let each one of you speak truth with his neighbor," for we are members of one another. 26 "Be angry, and do not sin": do not let the sun go down on your wrath, 27 nor give place to the devil. 28 Let him who stole steal no longer, but rather let him labor, working with his hands what is good, that he may have something to give him who has need. 29 Let no corrupt word proceed out of your mouth, but what is good for necessary edification, that it may impart grace to the hearers. 30 And do not grieve the Holy Spirit of God, by whom you were sealed for the day of redemption.*

In order to be used as a vessel for God our lifestyle must align with the Word of God. No amount of anointing oil poured over us will cleanse a life unfitting for the Master's use........There has to be transformation inwardly and outwardly.

Lesson 8

The Significance of the Anointing

<u>Isaiah 10: 24-27</u> **(cjb)** *Therefore ADONAI (sovereign) ELOHIM (triune)-Tzva'ot(Lord of Host) says: "My people living in <u>Tziyon</u>,(Zion) don't be afraid of Ashur,(Assyrian enemy) even when he strikes you with a stick and raises his staff against you, the way it was in Egypt. 25 For in but a little while, my fury will end; and my anger will have destroyed them." 26 ADONAI-Tzva'ot (sovereign Lord of Host) will wield a whip against them, as he did when striking Midyan at the Rock of 'Orev; as his staff was over the sea, he will raise it, the way it was in Egypt. 27 On that day his burden will fall from your shoulders and his yoke from your neck; the yoke will be destroyed by your (prosperity- Greek word – Shemen (translates-fruitfulness, richness which is a quality of the oil of olives)*

When Satan and his cohorts try to provoke us; harass us; steal from us; remove things from our lives, our ministry, our marriage, our children, our money etc., the Sovereign Triune Lord of Host will be upon us, like white on rice, to destroy all the enemies' yokes that have become a burden which kept us handcuffed and in bondage. Those yokes will be destroyed once and for all because of His mighty power and the power of His anointing. Praise the Lord!

Commit to Memory

- **Remember the Anointing is within us, declares 1 John 2:27** *But the anointing which you have received from Him abides in you, and you do not need that anyone teach you; but as the same anointing teaches you concerning all things, and is true, and is not a lie, and just as it has taught you, you will abide in Him.*

- **Remember the Anointing is Upon us declares Acts 1:8** *But you shall receive power when the Holy Spirit has come upon you;*

and you *shall be witnesses to Me in Jerusalem, and in all Judea and Samaria, and to the end of the earth."*

- <u>**Remind yourselves that Acts 10:38**</u> told us *how God anointed Jesus of Nazareth with the Holy Spirit and with power, who* **went** *about* **doing good** *and* **healing** *all who were oppressed by the devil, for God was with Him.* **So We too must Go - We too must do Good - We too must heal the Oppressed.**

<u>**Luke 4: 1, 18**</u> 1 *Then Jesus,* **being filled with the Holy Spirit**, *returned from the Jordan and was led by the Spirit into the wilderness,* (to test out His power). **We know that He was successful in triumphing over Satan because he makes a bold declaration in which He says"** *18 The* **Spirit of the Lord** *is upon Me (Jesus recognized that the God-head, the Father, the Spirit and the Word which He became was on the inside of him working together in perfect harmony to destroy the works of Satan) ; God has anointed Me; I will preach the gospel; I will heal what is broken; I will not only proclaim liberty I will set the captives free; I will restore vision to people without vision and I will free the oppressed.*

This is what the anointing looks like. This is what the anointing upon your life should look like!

A life that is free from sin, (**habitual sin, and practiced sin**) will be conducive to housing God's anointing and yielding to the ministry of the Holy Spirit. We will be sensitive to His unction's (inward witness, strong impression) and we will flow in His supernatural gifts.

Question 5: Do I need to be filled continually?
We only have to look to Elijah and Jesus for the answer.

<u>**Reflection: Read, Study and Discuss the following scriptures:**</u>

<u>**1Kings 19:4-8**</u> *But he himself went a day's journey into the wilderness, and came and sat down under a broom tree. And he prayed that he might die, and said, "It is enough! Now, Lord, take my life, for I am no better than my*

*fathers!"5 Then as he lay and slept under a broom tree, suddenly an angel touched him, and said to him, "**Arise and eat.**" 6 Then he looked, and there by his head was a cake baked on coals, and a jar of water. So he ate and drank, and lay down again. 7 And the angel of the Lord came back the second time, and touched him, and said, "**Arise and eat, because the journey is too great for you.**" 8 So he arose, and ate and drank; **and he went in the strength of that food forty days and forty nights as far as Horeb, the mountain of God.***

Luke 5:16 (cjb) *However, he made a practice of withdrawing to remote places in order to pray. **17** One day when Yeshua was teaching, there were P'rushim (Pharisees) and Torah-teachers present who had come from various villages in the Galil and Y'hudah, also from Yerushalayim; and* <u>*the power of ADONAI was with him to heal the sick.*</u> **Jesus had been refreshed after separating Himself to be empowered by the Spirit.**

John 17: 4-5 (cjb) *"I glorified **(honored, magnified)** you on earth by finishing the work you gave me to do. 5 Now, Father, **glorify me alongside yourself. Give me the same glory (dignity, praise, honor, worship) I had with you before the world existed.***

Jesus is praying for His spiritual position in the Godhead to be fully restored once His work has been completed as a man of flesh and bone. This is significant because as a **man facing death** he would soon be **reunited with the Father and Spirit in Deity.** He would no longer need His flesh and bone body which had its limitations to be powered from within. **After His resurrection He would be the source of Power.**

Matthew 26:36-45 (cjb) *Then Yeshua went with his talmidim* **(Disciples)** *to a place called Gat-Sh'manim (Gethsemane) and said to them, "Sit here while I go over there and pray." 37 He took with him Kefa **(Peter)** and Zavdai's (Zebedee) two sons. Grief and anguish came over him, 38 and he said to them, "My heart is so filled with sadness that I could die! Remain here and stay awake with me." 39 Going on a little farther, he fell on his face, praying, "My Father, if possible, let this cup pass from me! Yet -- not what I* *want, but what you want!"* **40** *He returned to the talmidim and found them sleeping. He said to Kefa,* **(Peter)** *"Were you so weak that you couldn't stay awake with me for even an hour?* **41** *Stay awake, and pray that you will not be put to the test -- the spirit indeed is eager, but human nature is weak."* **42** *A second time he went off and prayed. "My Father, if this cup cannot pass away unless I drink it, let what you want be done."* **43** *Again he returned and found them sleeping, their eyes were so heavy.* **44** *Leaving them again, he went off and prayed a third time, saying the same words.* **45** *Then he came to the talmidim and said, "For now, go on sleeping, take your rest. . . . Look! The time has come for the Son of Man to be betrayed into the hands of sinners.*

John 18: 4-6 *Yeshua, who knew everything that was going to happen to him, went out and asked them, "Whom do you want?" "Yeshua from* **5** *Natzeret," they answered. He said to them,* **"I AM." (I exist, have always been)** *Also standing with them was Y'hudah, the one who was betraying him.* **6** *When he said,* **"I AM ", they went back ward from him and fell to the ground. The anointing on Him was so strong and powerful, it knocked** the **soldiers off of their feet.**

The anointing on our lives is strong and powerful but Prayer is key to staying filled with the Spirit......Jude 20-23

Section 2

THE HOLY SPIRIT'S GIFT TO YOU

Joanne M. Green

66

Lesson 1

The Categories of Gifts

There are 3 categories of gifts

1. Holy Spirit's Gifts or Charismatic Gifts 1 Corinthians 12

- **Three Spoken Gifts**- diverse tongues; interpretation of tongues and prophecy
- **Three Power Gifts** – healing; working of miracles; faith
- **Three Revelation Gifts** – word of wisdom; word of knowledge; discerning of spirits

2. Ministerial Positions and Functionality - Ephesians 4:11

These offices or roles should be characterized by the fruits of the Spirit and several of the spiritual gifts. Not everyone functions in these offices or roles. These ministerial positions are usually demonstrated in a person's life but validated by God. **Romans 11:29 (cjb)** *says for God's free gifts and His calling are irrevocable; and are recognized by presbytery; presiding elders of a church body* as was the case with Timothy by Paul when he said in **Philippians 2:20-22** *But I trust in the Lord Jesus to send Timothy to you shortly, that I also may be encouraged when I know your state. 20 For I have no one like-minded, who will sincerely care for your state. 21 For all seek their own (some have their own agenda), not the things which are of Christ Jesus. 22 But you know his proven character, that as a son with his father he served with me in the gospel.*

- The role of the **Apostle** is to lay the foundation.
- The role of the **Prophet** is to be God's mouthpiece in the earth.
- The role of the **Evangelist** is to stir up people to win souls.
- The role of the **Pastor** is to shepherd and nurture the sheep.
- The role of the **Teacher** is to present Truth

3. Motivational Gifts

Romans 12

These gifts are for serving the body of Christ and are characterized by the fruits of the Spirit found in **Galatians 5:22** which are love, joy, peace, longsuffering, kindness, goodness, faithfulness, gentleness and self-control or temperance.

- There are seven motivational gifts (prophecy, serving, teaching, exhortation, giving, administration and mercy)
- Everyone has one dominant or strong motivational gift
- Motivational gifts are different from natural talents or abilities

Motivational gifts help us to identify others in the body of Christ and where they function.

There are three callings of God:

1. Call to Repentance
2. Call to Water Baptism
3. Call to Serve or function in the Body of Christ

The Bible says we are to *"know those that labor among you"*

Question: How does the Lord work with the Disciples?
<u>Mark 16:17-29</u> *And these signs will follow those who believe: In My name they will cast out demons;***(when casting out demons the revelation gifts will usually be in manifestation)** *they will speak with new tongues;***(when speaking in tongues the spoken gifts will usually be evident)** *18 they will take up serpents; and if they drink anything deadly, it will by no means hurt them;* **(the power gifts will usually be in manifestation)** *they will lay hands on the sick, and they will recover."***(***again* **the power gifts will be in manifestation)** *19 So then,*

after the Lord had spoken to them, He was received up into heaven, and sat down at the right hand of God. **20 And they went out and preached everywhere, the Lord working with them and confirming the word through the accompanying signs. We must not be a lone ranger or seek notoriety while being used by God. We must work in harmony with the Godhead!**

He sends the Holy Spirit – John 16:7 *Nevertheless I tell you the truth. It is to your advantage that I go away; for if I do not go away, the Helper will not come to you; but if I depart, I will send Him to you.* **In other words, the Holy Spirit, Ruach HaKodesh will come with His gifts to the believer to convert the unbelieving…..**

The gift of the Holy Spirit was not just given to those who were first to be filled. In **Acts 2: 38, 39** (cjb) *Kefa answered them, "Turn from sin, return to God, and each of you be immersed on the authority of Yeshua the Messiah into forgiveness of your sins, and* ***you will receive the gift of the Ruach HaKodesh!*** *39 For the promise is for you, for your children, and for those far away -* ***as many as ADONAI our God may call!***

REMEMBER: Jesus was also a "Man" in the earth operating under the power of the Holy Spirit in a limited measure.

Acts 10:38: God anointed Jesus with the Holy Spirit and with power, who went about doing good and *healing all who were oppressed* **by the devil, for God was with Him.**

Jesus was manifested or He was made evident in the flesh to destroy the works of Satan. Our works should be evident as believers that we have the power over the works of Satan, to destroy his works. **The Holy Spirit within us and upon us empowers and enables us to destroy those yokes of oppression. It's His anointing that is released in us…..Jesus called it virtue.**

Luke 5:16, 17 (cjb) Jesus made a practice of withdrawing to remote places in order to pray, so that the power of ADONAI our Sovereign

God would always be present to heal the sick. We too should be withdrawing to remote places to pray, so that the power of Adonai the sovereign God is present to heal the sick!

Chapter 11 of Luke teaches us how to pray and receive the things that we are petitioning God for. Luke concludes that we must be persistent in our asking in order to receive, by seeking we will find what we are looking for and by knocking nothing shall be withheld. **So Luke 11: 11-13** *refutes the idea that when we ask for the Holy Spirit and He becomes evident in our lives by the manifestation of His spiritual gifts which include tongues and the interpretation of tongues that what we have asked for comes from the devil....* **verses 14-23 further validates that line of thinking. The framework for Satan's kingdom is division......God's Kingdom is unified and is Greater!**

<u>**1 Corinthians 12:1 11 (cjb)**</u> tells us how to identify the Holy Spirit works by first telling us not to be ignorant about the things of the Spirit. And to be clear that no one speaking by the Spirit of God ever says, "Yeshua is cursed!" and no one can say, "Yeshua is Lord," except by the **Ruach HaKodesh.** There are different kinds of gifts, but the Holy Spirit dispenses them. There are different ways of serving, but it is the Lord that is being served. There are different modes of working, but it is God working them all in everyone. Each person is given the particular manifestation of the Spirit that will be for the common good. **(To work in harmony – not in competition)**

The Holy Spirit will give to one a **word of wisdom**; to another, a **word of knowledge** in accordance with the His Spirit; to another, **faith,** to another **gifts of healing**; to another the **working of miracles;** to another **prophecy**; to another the **ability to judge** (discern) between spirits; to another *the* **ability to speak in different kinds of tongues and yet another the ability to interpret tongues.** *He is One and the same Spirit who is at work in all of these manifestations distributing to each person as He chooses.*

These nine spiritual gifts can be easily remembered by the following:

Three Spoken Gifts-**(they are heard)** diverse tongues; interpretation of tongues and prophecy

Three Power Gifts **(they are demonstrated)** – healing; working of miracles; faith

Three Revelation Gifts **(they are intuitive; divine insight)** – word of wisdom; word of knowledge; discerning of spirits

Lesson 2

The Gift of Wisdom

Let's look at each gift individually

<u>What is the Word of Wisdom</u> –it is a supernatural revelation from God pointing to the future. It might be audible; visionary or given in a dream. It includes the mind, the will and purpose of God. **This gift should not be confused with natural wisdom.**

<u>Natural Wisdom - James 3: 13-17</u> *Who among you is wise and understanding? Let him demonstrate it by his good way of life, by actions done in the humility that grows out of wisdom. 14 But if you harbor in your hearts bitter jealousy and selfish ambition, don't boast and attack the truth with lies! 15 This wisdom is not the kind that comes down from above; on the contrary, it is worldly, unspiritual, and demonic. 16 For where there are jealousy and selfish ambition, there will be disharmony and every foul practice. 17 But the wisdom from above is, first of all, pure, then peaceful, kind, open to reason, full of mercy and good fruits, without partiality and without hypocrisy.*

Examples of Word of Wisdom:

<u>Ananias - Acts 9: 10-16</u> Now there was a certain disciple at Damascus named Ananias; and to him the Lord said in a vision, "Ananias." And he said, "Here I am, Lord." **11** So the Lord said to him, *"Arise and go to the street called Straight, and inquire at the house of Judas for one called Saul of Tarsus, for behold, he is praying. 12 And in a vision he has seen a man named Ananias coming in and putting his hand on him, so that he might receive his sight."* **13** *Then Ananias answered, "Lord, I have heard from many about this man, how much harm he has done to Your saints in Jerusalem. 14 And here he has authority from the chief priests to bind all who call on Your name." 15 But the Lord said to him, "Go, for he is a chosen vessel of Mine to bear My name before Gentiles,*

kings, and the *children of Israel. 16 For I will show him how many things he must suffer for My name's sake.*

Joseph - Genesis 37:5-11 Joseph had a dream, and he told it to his brothers; and they hated him even more. **6** So he said to them, ***"Please hear this dream which I have dreamed: 7 There we were, binding sheaves in the field. Then behold, my sheaf arose and also stood upright; and indeed your sheaves stood all around and bowed down to my sheaf."* 8** And his brothers said to him, *"Shall you indeed reign over us? Or shall you indeed have dominion over us?" So they hated him even more for his dreams and for his words.* **9 Then he dreamed still another dream and told it to his brothers, and said, "Look, I have dreamed another dream. And this time, the sun, the moon, and the eleven stars bowed down to me."10** *So he told it to his father and his brothers; and his father rebuked him and said to him, "What is this dream that you have dreamed? Shall your mother and I and your brothers indeed come to bow down to the earth before you?"* **11** *And his brothers envied him, but his father kept the matter in mind.*

So far, we read about two individuals that were given the Word of Wisdom to reveal future events and how they looked in a practical sense. Ananias was given a Word of Wisdom regarding Paul's conversion and future ministry in Acts 9: 10-16 **and Joseph was given a Word of Wisdom regarding his future through a dream in** Genesis 37: 5-11

Let's look at other examples of the Word of Wisdom:

Acts 21:4-36 **(I will just make reference to the verses that are specific to the word of wisdom)**

4 ***And finding disciples, we stayed there seven days. They told Paul through the Spirit not to go up to Jerusalem. The disciples had a word of wisdom regarding harm that would befall Paul if he went to Jerusalem...*** 5 *When we had come to the end of those days, we departed and went on our way; and they all accompanied us, with wives and children, till we were out of the city. And we knelt down on the shore and prayed.* 6

When we had taken our leave of one another, we boarded the ship, and they returned home. 7 *And when we had finished our voyage from Tyre, we came to Ptolemais, greeted the brethren, and stayed with them one day.* **8 On the next day we who were Paul's companions departed and came to Caesarea, and entered the house of Philip the evangelist, who was one of the seven, and stayed with him. 9 Now this man had four virgin daughters who prophesied. 10 And as we stayed many days, a certain prophet named Agabus came down from Judea. 11 When he had come to us, he took Paul's belt, bound his own hands and feet, and said, "Thus says the Holy Spirit, 'So shall the Jews at Jerusalem bind the man who owns this belt, and deliver him into the hands of the Gentiles.' "12 Now when we heard these things, both we and those from that place pleaded with him not to go up to Jerusalem. 13 Then Paul answered, "What do you mean by weeping and breaking my heart? For I am ready not only to be bound, but also to die at Jerusalem for the name of the Lord Jesus." 14 So when he would not be persuaded, we ceased, saying, "The will of the Lord be done."**

15 *And after those days we packed and went up to Jerusalem.* **16** *Also some of the disciples from Caesarea went with us and brought with them a certain Manson of Cyprus, an early disciple, with whom we were to lodge. 17 And when we had come to Jerusalem, the brethren received us gladly.* **18** On the following day Paul went in with us to James, and all the elders were present. 19 When he had greeted them, he told in detail those things which God had done among the Gentiles through his ministry. 26 Then Paul took the men, and the next day, having been purified with them, entered the temple to announce the expiration of the days of purification, at which time an offering should be made for each one of them. **27** *Now when the seven days were almost ended, the Jews from Asia, seeing him in the temple, stirred up the whole crowd and laid hands on him,* **28** *crying out, "Men of Israel, help! This is the man who teaches all men everywhere against the people, the law, and this place; and furthermore he also brought Greeks into the temple and has defiled this holy place."* **29** *For they had previously seen Trophimus the Ephesian with him in the city, whom they supposed that Paul had brought into the temple.* **30** *And all the city was* *disturbed; and the people ran together, seized Paul, and dragged him out of the temple; and immediately the doors were shut. 31 Now as they were seeking to kill him, news came to the commander of the garrison that all Jerusalem was in an uproar. 32 He immediately took soldiers and centurions, and ran down to them. And when they saw the commander and the soldiers, they stopped beating Paul. 33 Then the commander came near and took him, and commanded him to be bound with two chains; and he asked who he was and what he had done. 34 And some among the multitude cried one thing and some another. So when he could not ascertain the truth because of the tumult, he commanded him to be taken into the barracks. 35 When he reached the stairs, he had to be carried by the soldiers because of the violence of the mob. 36 For the multitude of the people followed after, crying out, "Away with him!"*

Note: Paul was warned twice about the trouble he would encounter, but he made a decision not be deterred in his preaching the gospel and ministering to the Gentiles. It was his decision and God allowed it. Some decisions that we make after having received a word of wisdom God will allow and He will work it together for our good.

Acts 27: 6-44

Here is an example of the word of wisdom and counsel not heeded by those to whom it was given……..

6 There the centurion found an Alexandrian ship sailing to Italy, and he put us on board. 7 When we had sailed slowly many days, and arrived with difficulty off Cnidus, the wind not permitting us to proceed, we sailed under the shelter of Crete off Salmone. 8 Passing it with difficulty, we came to a place called Fair Havens, near the city of Lasea. 9 Now when much time had been spent, and sailing was now dangerous because the Fast was already over, Paul advised them, 10 saying, "Men, I perceive that this voyage will end with disaster and much loss, not only of the cargo and ship, but also our lives." 11 Nevertheless the centurion was more persuaded by the helmsman and the owner of the ship than by the things spoken by Paul. The helmsman or ship's captain ignored the instructions of

Paul- this was clearly a warning. **12** And because the harbor was not suitable to winter in, the majority advised to set sail from there also, if by any means they could reach Phoenix, a harbor of Crete opening toward the southwest and northwest, and winter there. **13** When the south wind blew softly, supposing that they had obtained their desire, putting out to sea, they sailed close by Crete. **14** *But not long after, a tempestuous head wind arose, called Euroclydon.* **15** *So when the ship was caught, and could not head into the wind, we let her drive.* **16** And running under the shelter of an island called Clauda, we secured the skiff with difficulty. **17** When they had taken it on board, they used cables to undergird the ship; and fearing lest they should run aground on the Syrtis Sands, they struck sail and so were driven. **18 And because we were exceedingly tempest-tossed, the next day** *they lightened the ship.* **19** *On the third day we threw the ship's tackle overboard with our own hands.* **20** *Now when neither sun nor stars appeared for many days, and no small tempest beat on us, all hope that we would be saved was finally given up.* **21** *But after long abstinence from food, then Paul stood in the midst of them and said, "Men, you should have listened to me, and not have sailed from Crete and incurred this disaster and loss.* **22** *And now I urge you to take heart, for there will be no loss of life among you, but only of the ship.* **23** *For there stood by me this night an angel of the God to whom I belong and whom I serve,* **24** *saying, 'Do not be afraid, Paul; you must be brought before Caesar; and indeed God has granted you all those who sail with you.'* **25** *Therefore take heart, men, for I believe God that it will be just as it was told me.* **26** *However, we must run aground on a certain island."* **27** *Now when the fourteenth night had come, as we were driven up and down in the Adriatic Sea, about midnight the sailors sensed that they were drawing near some land.* **28** *And they took soundings and found it to be twenty fathoms; and when they had gone a little farther, they took soundings again and found it to be fifteen fathoms.* **29** *Then, fearing lest we should run aground on the rocks, they dropped four anchors from the stern, and prayed for day to come.* **30** *And as the sailors were seeking to escape from the ship, when they had let down the skiff into the sea, under pretense of putting out anchors from the prow,* **31 Paul said to the centurion and the soldiers, "Unless these men stay in the ship,** *you cannot be saved." Paul reminding them of the original instructions. 32 Then the soldiers cut away the ropes of the skiff and let it fall off. 33 And as day was about to dawn, Paul implored them all to take food, saying, "Today is the fourteenth day you have waited and continued without food, and eaten nothing. 34 Therefore I urge you to take nourishment, for this is for your survival, <u>since not a hair will fall from the head of any of you."</u>35 And when he had said these things, he took bread and gave thanks to God in the presence of them all; and when he had broken it he began to eat. 36 Then they were all encouraged, and also took food themselves. 37 And in all we were two hundred and seventy-six persons on the ship. 38 So when they had eaten enough, they lightened the ship and threw out the wheat into the sea. 39 When it was day, they did not recognize the land; but they observed a bay with a beach, onto which they planned to run the ship if possible. 42 And the soldiers' plan was to kill the prisoners, lest any of them should swim away and escape. 43 But the centurion, wanting to save Paul, kept them from their purpose, and commanded that those who could swim should jump overboard first and get to land, 44 and the rest, some on boards and some on parts of the ship. And so it was that they all escaped safely to land.*

Again a decision was made to travel even when warned by a word of wisdom not too....It should be very clear to us that God will never override the will of man......and as it was the case of Adam.

In the Old Testament, we have to remember since the Holy Spirit was not yet released God used prophets, dreams, visions and at times He himself spoke audibly to His servants. In some instances the **Word of Wisdom can be conditional as in the case of Hezekiah.**

<u>2 Kings 20 (also found in Isaiah 38)</u> *In those days Hezekiah was sick and near death. And Isaiah the prophet, the son of Amoz, went to him and said to him, "Thus says the Lord: 'Set your house in order, for you shall die, and not live.' " 2 Then he turned his face toward the wall, and prayed to the Lord, saying, 3 "Remember now, O Lord, I pray, how I have walked before You in truth and with a loyal heart, and have done what was good in Your sight." And Hezekiah wept bitterly. 4 And it happened,*

before Isaiah had gone out into the middle court, that the word of the Lord came to him, saying, 5 "Return and tell Hezekiah the leader of My people, 'Thus says the Lord, the God of David your father: "I have heard your prayer, I have seen your tears; surely I will heal you. On the third day you shall go up to the house of the Lord. 6 And I will add to your days fifteen years. I will deliver you and this city from the hand of the king of Assyria; and I will defend this city for My own sake, and for the sake of My servant David." 7 Then Isaiah said, "Take a lump of figs." So they took and laid it on the boil, and he recovered. 8 And Hezekiah said to Isaiah, "What is the sign that the Lord will heal me, and that I shall go up to the house of the Lord the third day?" 9 Then Isaiah *said,* **"This is the sign to you from the Lord, that the Lord will do the thing which He has spoken: shall the shadow go forward ten degrees or go backward ten degrees?" 10 And Hezekiah answered, "It is an easy thing for the shadow to go down ten degrees; no, but let the shadow go backward ten degrees." 11 So Isaiah the prophet cried out to the Lord, and He brought the shadow ten degrees backward, by which it had gone down on the sundial of Ahaz. This is clearly a Word of Wisdom and a Working of a Miracle in manifestation. 12** *At that time Berodach-Baladan the son of Baladan, king of Babylon, sent letters and a present to Hezekiah, for he heard that Hezekiah had been sick.* **The King of Babylon was sending spies and not ambassadors.** *13 And Hezekiah was attentive to them, and showed them all the house of his treasures--the silver and gold, the spices and precious ointment, and all his armory--all that was found among his treasures.* **There was nothing in his house or in all his dominion that Hezekiah did not show them. 14** *Then Isaiah the prophet went to King Hezekiah, and said to him, "What did these men say, and from where did they come to you?" So Hezekiah said, "They came from a far country, from Babylon." 15 And he said, "What have they seen in your house?" So Hezekiah answered, "They have seen all that is in my house; there is nothing among my treasures that I have not shown them."* **16 Then Isaiah said to Hezekiah, "Hear the word of the Lord: (2nd word of wisdom)**

17 'Behold, the days are coming when all that is in your house, and what your fathers have accumulated until this day, shall be carried to Babylon;

nothing shall be left,' says the Lord. **18** *'And they shall take away some of your sons who will descend from you, whom you will beget; and they shall be eunuchs in the palace of the king of Babylon.* **19** *Hezekiah said to Isaiah, "The word of the Lord which you have spoken is good!" For he said, "Will there not be peace and truth at least in my days?"*

Hezekiah's mistake was he was prideful and that he exposed the tribe of Judah wealth and security to the enemies of Babylon. His punishment was just in that he would not have a righteous seed to sit on his throne. Manasseh was very evil and did not follow the ways of his father. He reinstituted Baal idol worship.

Personal Study: Review Acts 9 and try to identify any other gift of the Spirit that accompanied the Word of Wisdom.

Lesson 3

The Gift of Knowledge

REVIEW ~ RUMINATE ~ REFLECT

<u>Acts 10:38</u>: *God anointed Jesus with the Holy Spirit and with power, who went about doing good and **healing all who were oppressed** by the devil, for God was with Him.*

Jesus was manifested to destroy the works of Satan. As spirit filled believers our ministry work should be to demonstrate the Holy Spirits power in order to destroy his works. The anointing released in us is called His virtue.

<u>**Gifts of the Holy Spirit   1 Corinthians 12:1- 11**</u>

There are nine spiritual gifts: three which are Spoken Gifts-(they are heard) diverse tongues; interpretation of tongues and prophecy; **three which are Power Gifts** (they are demonstrated) – healing; working of miracles; faith and **three which are Revelatory Gifts** (they are divinely intuitive) – word of wisdom; word of knowledge; discerning of spirits

The Word of Wisdom is a supernatural revelation from God pointing to the future. It might be audible; visionary or given in a dream. It includes the mind, the will and purpose of God and should not be confused with man's natural wisdom found in **James 3: 13-17**

<u>**Personal Study:**</u> In the previous lesson you were asked to review **Acts 9** once again to identify any other gifts of the Spirit that accompanied the **Word of Wisdom.**

The **Word of Wisdom** is clearly outlined in **verses 15, 16** because the plan and purpose of God for Paul was revealed. The **Word of Knowledge** is the second gift outlined in **verses 10-12**. These two gifts will almost always flow together in an individual that yields to the

Holy Spirit's leading for ministry. **Verse 18** reveals the **gift of healing** manifested to remove the scales from Paul's eyes. **Verse 32-35** reveals the **gift of healing** for Aeneas and in **Verse 36-40** the **working of miracles** is manifested to raise Dorcas from the dead.

The Word of Knowledge

The Word of Knowledge is a supernatural revelation from God specifically pertaining to facts or events. It can be manifested through a vision; given as spiritual enlightenment or inward revelation. The **Word of Knowledge** gives revelation about things past or present, it is never revelation of the future.

Remember the Word of Knowledge is always revelation given about specific information regarding ones past or present state. Now take look at **Acts 9:10-12**; here you have information about the person Saul of Tarsus and his whereabouts, the street called Straight; the house of Judas is the specific location; as well as Saul would be praying. All of this information refers to present facts.

Let's look at some examples of the Word of Knowledge in the Old Testament and the New Testament

Old Testament

2 Kings 5:25-27 (cjb) You will discover three gifts in manifestation:

Verse 25, 26 - the gift of Discernment by Elisha

Verse 26b - the Word of Knowledge

Verse 27 - the gift of Prophecy

2 Kings 5: 15 *Then, with his whole retinue, he returned to the man of God, went and stood before him, and said, "Well, I've learned that there is no God in all the earth except in Isra'el; therefore, please accept a present from your servant."* **16** *But Elisha answered, "As ADONAI lives, before whom I stand,* **I will not accept it." And despite his urging him to take it, he refused. Elisha gives God the Glory and Honor for Naaman's healing and resolved within himself not be rewarded for the miracle.** **17** *So Na'aman said, "If you won't take it, then please let your servant be given as much earth as two mules can carry; because from now on, your servant will offer neither burnt offerings nor sacrifices to other gods, but only to* ADONAI. **Naaman had respect and acknowledges Elisha's God, the One True God as the One God he will begin to worship. Naaman had a heart conversion. We must remember that the gifts of the Holy Spirit are manifested to win the hearts of unbelievers.** **18** *Except this, and may ADONAI forgive your servant for it: when my master goes into the temple of Rimmon to worship there, and he leans on my hand, and I bow down in the temple of Rimmon - when I bow down, may ADONAI forgive your servant for this."* **Naaman wanted assurance from Elisha that since he was a man under authority to his master, that God, would forgive him of his obedience to serve his natural master. We too are under authority and must obey those who have rule over us. Naaman had a true heart conversion but it did not change the fact that he was employed by a master to whom he was obligated to obey. Elisha extends the Peace of God which was an assurance that all would be well. God extends His Grace over our lives when we find ourselves in similar situations on our jobs and settings that require us to obey those who rule over us.** **19** *Elisha said to him, "Go in peace." Na'aman had gone only a short distance from him,* **20** *when Geichazi, the servant of Elisha the man of God, said to himself, "Here, my master has made it easy on this Arami Na'aman by not accepting from him what he brought. As ADONAI lives, I'll run after him and get at least something from him."* **21** *So Geichazi hurried off after Na'aman. When Na'aman saw someone running after him, he got down from his chariot to meet him and asked, "Is* *everything all* right?"**22** *"Yes," he replied. "My master sent me with this message: 'Two young men have just now come to me, guild prophets from the hills of Efrayim. Would you be kind enough to give them a talent of silver [sixty-six pounds] and two changes of clothes?"* **23** *"By all means, take two talents!" said Na'aman, pressing him. He tied up the two talents of silver in two bags and gave them, with the two changes of clothes, to two of his servants, who carried them ahead of Geichazi.* **Geichazi's true nature is revealed. His character is founded in deception and greed. God says in Jeremiah 17:9, 10 that the heart of man is deceitful and desperately wicked. God tries our hearts and we are rewarded with the fruits of our doing. Geichazi sin does not go unnoticed or unpunished.** **24** On reaching the hill, he took the bags from them and put them away in the house. Then he let the men go, and they left. **25** *He went in and stood before his master. Elisha asked, "Where have you been, Geichazi?" "Your servant hasn't gone anywhere," he said.* **26** *Elisha said to him, "Wasn't my heart there with you when the man left his chariot to meet you? Is this a time to receive silver and clothing - and olive groves and vineyards and sheep and oxen and male and female slaves?* **27** Therefore Na'aman's tzara'at (**Leprosy**) will cling to you and your descendants forever." He left Elisha's presence with tzara'at (**Leprosy**) as white as snow. **The gift of discernment and the gift of prophecy can be clearly observed.**

2 Kings 6: 8-12 (cjb) the Word of Knowledge was given to warn the King of Israel regarding the plans of his enemy the King of Syria

8 *Now the king of Aram went to war against Isra'el; and in consulting his servants he said, "I'll set up my ambush camp in such-and-such a place."* **9** *The man of God sent this message to the king of Isra'el: "Be careful not to go past such-and-such a place, because Aram will attack there."* **10** *So the king of Isra'el sent men to the place the man of God had told him and warned him about, and he took special precautions there. This happened more than once or twice,* **11** *and it greatly upset the king of Aram. He called his servants and* *said to them, "Tell me which of you is betraying us to the king of* Isra'el?"**12** *One of his servants replied, "It's not that, my lord, king. Rather, Elisha, the prophet who is in Isra'el, tells the king of Isra'el the words you speak privately in your own bedroom!"*

1 Samuel 9: 3-6; 15-20 (cjb)   the Word of Knowledge was given to recover lost property belonging to Samuel and Saul, as well as a Word of Knowledge from God to Samuel

*3 Once the donkeys belonging to Kish Sha'ul's **(Saul's)** father got lost. Kish said to his son Sha'ul, "Please take one of the servants with you, go out, and look for the donkeys." 4 He went through the hills of Efrayim and the territory of Shalishah, but they didn't find them. Then they went through the territory of Sha'alim, but they weren't there. They went through the territory of Binyamin but didn't find them there either. 5 On reaching the territory of Tzuf, (Zuph) Sha'ul said to his servant with him, "Come, let's go back; otherwise my father will stop thinking about the donkeys and start worrying about us." 6 His servant replied, "Here now, there's a man of God in this city, a man who is highly respected, and everything he says proves true. Let's go to him; maybe he can tell us something about where we should go. They went up to the city; and as they entered the city, there was Sh'mu'el coming out toward them to go up to the high place. 15 The day before Sha'ul arrived, ADONAI **(Sovereign God)** had given Sh'mu'el a revelation: 16 "Tomorrow at about this time I will send you a man from the territory of Binyamin. You are to anoint him prince over my people Isra'el. He will save my people from the power of the P'lishtim, (Philistines) because I have seen my people's situation, and their cry of distress has come to me."* **This is a Word of Knowledge being given by the Prophet Samuel.** *17 When Sh'mu'el saw Sha'ul, ADONAI said to him, "Here is the man I told you about, the one who is going to govern my people." 18 Sha'ul approached Sh'mu'el in the gateway and said, "Please tell me where the seer's house is." 19 Sh'mu'el answered Sha'ul, "I'm the seer. Go up ahead of me to the high place, because you are going to dine with me today. In the morning, I will let you leave; and I will tell you everything that is on your heart. 20 As for your donkeys that got lost three days ago, don't worry about* *them*; they've been found. **Again the Word of Knowledge being given to Saul by the Prophet Samuel.**

New Testament

Reflection and Personal Study: Read Acts 10: 9-33

<u>Acts 10:9-20, 30-33</u> Peter had a vision before he had a **Word of Knowledge**; a **Word of Knowledge** was given to Cornelius to bring him and his household to salvation.

Verses 9-16 - The vision of Peter regarding the Gentiles being brought to salvation which includes Cornelieus.

Verse 17 - **Word of Knowledge** given to Peter.

Verse 30-33 - Explanation of the **Word of Knowledge** by Cornelius.

Lesson 4

The Gift of Discernment

REVIEW ~ RUMINATE ~ REFLECT

<u>Acts 10:38</u> *God anointed Jesus with the Holy Spirit and with power, who went about doing good and* **healing all who were oppressed** *by the devil, for God was with Him.*

<u>Gifts of the Holy Spirit 1 Corinthians 12:1- 11</u>

There are nine spiritual gifts: three which are Spoken Gifts - diverse tongues; interpretation of tongues and prophecy; **three which are Power Gifts** - healing; working of miracles; faith **and three which are Revelatory Gifts** – word of wisdom; word of knowledge; discerning of spirits.

The Word of Wisdom is a supernatural revelation from God pointing to the future. It might be audible; visionary or given in a dream. It includes the mind, the will and purpose of God and should not be confused with man's natural wisdom found in **<u>James 3: 13-17.</u>**

The Word of Knowledge is a supernatural revelation from God specifically pertaining to facts or events. It can be manifested through a vision; given as spiritual enlightenment or inward revelation. The **Word of Knowledge** gives revelation about things past or present, it is never revelation of the future.

<u>In 2 Kings 5:25-27</u> we found three gifts in manifestation: verse 25, 26 gift of discernment by Elisha, word of knowledge verse 26b and prophecy verse 27

25 Geichazi came back from a visit with Naaman He went in and stood before his master. Elisha asked, "Where have you been, Geichazi?" "His reply to his master was that he had not gone anywhere. Your servant hasn't gone anywhere," he said. **26** Elisha said to him, "Wasn't my heart there with you when the man left his chariot to meet you? Is this a time to receive silver and clothing - and olive groves and vineyards and sheep and oxen and male and female slaves?

In the previous verses of scripture we observe Elisha demonstrating the **gift of discernment** when confronting Geichazi regarding **the spirit of deception and the spirit of greed**. We know what the gift looks like but not how we define it. We also want to talk about what the **spirit of discernment is and what it is not.**

The Discerning of Spirits is supernatural revelation or insight from God to identify activity in the realm of the spirit in situations or circumstances. **Spiritual discernment** is not reading the mind but rather identifying the activity that is promoted and or demonstrated by demonic spirits. This is not a natural feeling or knowing. It is formulated in your spirit not in your soul (mind, will, emotions).

Things to know about the gift of discernment:

1. There is no distance when we operate in the spirit. Geographical locations are not restricted or limited to dethroning or cancelling the assignments of these spirits. **In 2 Kings 5:25, 26,** Elisha was not in the same locale as Geichazi to identify the spirit activity that was taking place. Elisha **identified the "spirit of greed"** had manifested as well as, **discerned the intent of Geichazi's heart (deception)** which was to use the money he had received from Naaman to buy olive groves, vineyards and flocks and servants.

2. There are four classes of rebel or evil spirits:

- **Wicked spirits in high places** - wicked spirits of Satan operating specifically in the heavenlies.
- **Rulers of darkness of this world** - these are the most intelligent and spirit world rulers, like Hitler, Saadam Hussein, ISIS, and Gadhafi etc.

- **Principalities** - regional- territorial- chief rulers or beings of the highest rank and order in Satan's kingdom (Example: San Francisco spirit of homosexuality; Louisiana spirit of witchcraft)
- **Powers -** those demon spirits that derive their power from and execute the will of the chief rulers (Example: Legion was a demon spirit comprised of many spirits who oppressed the man of the Gadarenes found in **Mark 5**).

NOTE: Colossians 2:9, 10, 15 (cjb)

*9 For in him, bodily, lives the fullness of all that God is. 10 And it is in union with him that you have been made full - he is the head of every rule and authority. 15 **Stripping the rulers and authorities of their power, he made a public spectacle of them, triumphing over them by means of the stake.***

3. These spirits gain entrance through the doorway of your mind.

The Discerning of Spirits is supernatural revelation or insight from God to identify activity in the realm of the spirit in situations or circumstances.

Act 13:6-10 *Now when they (Barnabas, Paul and John) had gone through the island to Paphos, they found a **certain sorcerer, a false prophet,** a Jew whose name was Bar-Jesus, 7 who was with the proconsul, Sergius Paulus, an intelligent man. This man called for Barnabas and Saul and sought to hear the word of God. 8 But Elymas the sorcerer (for so his name is translated) withstood them, seeking to turn the proconsul away from the faith. 9 **Then Saul, who also is called Paul, filled with the Holy Spirit, looked intently at him 10 and said,*** "O full of all deceit and all fraud, you son of the devil, you enemy of all righteousness, will you not cease perverting the straight ways of the Lord?

Paul was operating under the power of the Holy Spirit who was able to discern the demonic activity of Elymas the sorcerer.

Acts 16:16-18

16 Now it happened as we went to prayer that a certain slave girl possessed with a spirit of divination met us, who brought her masters much profit by fortune telling. 17 This girl followed Paul and us, and cried out saying, "These men are the servants of the Most High God who proclaim to us the way of salvation" 18 And this she did for many days, but Paul greatly annoyed, turned and said to the spirit, I command you in the name of Jesus Christ to come out of her. And he came out that very hour.

Additional Examples:

John 2:25   (cjb)

25 that is, Jesus, he didn't need anyone to inform him about a person, because he knew what was in the person's heart.

Jesus being filled and baptized with the Holy Spirit "as a man" was able to discern the intents of the heart.

Matthew 9: 1-6 (cjb)

1 So he stepped into a boat, crossed the lake again and came to his own town. **2** Some people brought him a paralyzed man lying on a mattress. When Yeshua saw their trust, he said to the paralyzed man, "Courage, son! Your sins are forgiven." **3** On seeing this, some of the Torah-teachers said among themselves, "This man is blaspheming!" **4 Yeshua, knowing what they were thinking,** said, "Why are you entertaining evil thoughts in your hearts? **5** Tell me, which is easier to say `Your sins are forgiven' or `Get up and walk'?

Note: It is unwise to operate outside of your gifting. The following scripture is an example of the consequences.

Acts 19:11-16

11 Now God worked unusual miracles by the hands of Paul, 12 so that even handkerchiefs or aprons were brought from his body to the sick, and the diseases left them and the evil spirits went out of them. **13** *Then some of the itinerant Jewish exorcists took it upon themselves to call the name of the Lord Jesus over those who had evil spirits, saying, "We exorcise you by the Jesus whom Paul preaches."* **14** *Also there were seven sons of Sceva, a Jewish chief priest, who did so.* **15** *And the evil spirit answered and said, "Jesus I know, and Paul I know; but who are you?"* **16** *Then the man in whom the evil spirit was leaped on them, overpowered them, and prevailed against them, so that they fled out of that house naked and wounded.*

Personal Study: Identify the type of demonic spirit activity in the following scriptures. We will discuss these scriptures in the next lesson.

Mark 5:1-5

Mark 1:32-34

Luke 4:40-41

Matthew 9:32-34

Lesson 5

The Gift of Healing

REVIEW ~ RUMINATE ~ REFLECT

<u>Acts 10:38</u> *God anointed Jesus with the Holy Spirit and with power, who went about doing good and* **healing all who were oppressed** *by the devil, for God was with Him.* **The gifts of the Holy Spirit were not just for Jesus and His disciples. The gifts are manifested as a sign to the unbeliever according to** <u>1 Corinthians 14</u>.

<u>Gifts of the Holy Spirit 1 Corinthians 12:1- 11</u>

<u>There are nine spiritual gifts:</u> **three which are Spoken Gifts** - diverse tongues; interpretation of tongues and prophecy; **three which are Power Gifts** - healing; working of miracles; faith and **three which are Revelatory Gifts** – word of wisdom; word of knowledge; discerning of spirits.

The Word of Wisdom is a supernatural revelation from God pointing to the future. It might be audible; visionary or given in a dream. It includes the mind, the will and purpose of God and should not be confused with man's natural wisdom found in **<u>James 3: 13-17.</u>**

The Word of Knowledge is a supernatural revelation from God specifically pertaining to facts or events. The **Word of Knowledge** also gives revelation about things past or present, it is never revelation of the future. It can be manifested through a vision; given as spiritual enlightenment or inward revelation.

The Discerning of Spirits is supernatural revelation or insight from God to identify activity in the realm of the spirit in situations or circumstances. Spiritual discernment is not reading the mind but rather identifying the activity that is promoted and or demonstrated by demonic spirits. This is not a natural feeling or knowing. It is formulated in your spirit not in your soul (mind, will, emotions)

Things to know about the gift of discernment

1. There is no distance when we operate in the spirit. Geographical locations are not restricted or limited to dethroning or cancelling the assignments of these spirits. **Refer to 2 Kings 5:25, 26**,

2. There are four classes of rebel or evil spirits: Ephesians 6:12

- **Wicked spirits in high places** (wicked spirits of Satan operating specifically in the heavenlies)
- **Rulers of darkness of this world** (these are the most intelligent and spirit world rulers, like Hitler, Saadam Hussein, ISIS, Gadhafi etc.)
- **Principalities** (regional- territorial- chief rulers or beings of the highest rank and order in Satan's kingdom) San Francisco spirit of homosexuality; Louisiana spirit of witchcraft
- Powers (those demon spirits that derive their power from and execute the will of the chief rulers (Legion in Mark 5-the man of the Gadarenes)

3. These spirits gain entrance through the doorway of your mind

Here are examples of the Discerning of Spirits found in the following scriptures:

Acts 13: 6-10 or Acts 16: 16-18, and **Matthew 9:1-6**

Let's take a look together at Acts 16:16-18 (nkjv)

16 *Now it happened as we went to prayer that a certain slave girl possessed with a* **spirit of divination (python spirit)** *met us, who brought her masters much profit by fortune telling.* **17** *This girl followed Paul and us, and cried out saying, "These men are the servants of the Most High God who proclaim to us the way of salvation" And this she did for many days, but Paul greatly annoyed, turned and said to the spirit, I command you in the name of Jesus Christ to come out of her. And he came out that very hour.*

Acts 16:16-18 (cjb)
Once, when we were going to the place where the minyan (number) gathered, we were met by a **slave girl** *(she is oppressed by these spirits) who had in her a* **snake-spirit** *(spirit of python) that enabled her to predict the future. She earned a lot of money for her owners by telling fortunes.* **17** *This girl followed behind Sha'ul and the rest of us and kept screaming, "These men are servants of God Ha'Elyon! They're telling you how to be saved!"* **(Also a familiar spirit or religious spirit agitated Paul)** **18** *She kept this up day after day, until Sha'ul, greatly disturbed, turned and said to the spirit, "In the name of Yeshua the Messiah, I order you to come out of her!" And the spirit did come out, at that very moment*

Personal Study: In the previous lesson you were to identify the spirit activity in the following scriptures which was an exercise using the **gift of discernment.**

Mark 5: 1-15
Mark 1: 32-34
Luke 4: 40-41
Matthew 9:32-34

Personal Study –Answer to Mark 5:1-15 (cjb)

Yeshua and his talmidim (disciples) arrived at the other side of the lake, in the Gerasenes' territory. 2 As soon as he disembarked, a man with an **unclean spirit (an unclean spirit is a spirit that is demonic and evil in nature, will possess and torment the individual it is housed in and demonstrates lewd behavior)***, came out of the burial caves to meet him. 3 He lived in the burial caves; and no one could keep him tied up, not even with a chain. 4 He had often been chained hand and foot, but he would snap the chains and break the irons off his feet, and* **no one was strong enough to control him.**_*5 Night and day he wandered among the graves and through the hills, howling and gashing himself with stones. 6 Seeing Yeshua from a distance, he ran and fell on his knees in front of him 7 and screamed at the top of his voice,* **"What do you want with me, Yeshua, Son of God Ha`Elyon?** *I implore you in God's name! Don't torture me!"* **(This is a religious spirit that is in manifestation. A Religious spirit has head knowledge about God but no relationship with God, it is almost always legalistic , holding on to man's traditions and doctrines or dogmas)** *8 For Yeshua had already begun saying to him,* **"Unclean spirit, and come out of this man!"** *9 Yeshua asked him,* **"What's your name?"** **"My name is Legion,"** *he answered,* **"there are so many of us";** *10 and he kept begging Yeshua not to send them out of that region.* **(Legion is defined as a chief subdivision of the Roman army, containing anywhere from 3000 to 6000 infantry, with a contingent of cavalry. The term does not occur in the Bible in its primary sense, but appears to have been adopted in order to express any large number of demonic spirits who operate in order of rank and subordination to their master spirits. In this case Legion formed an alliance with other spirits to rule in power and govern as a principality in this region and did not want to give up this territory.** *(11 Now there was a large herd of pigs feeding near the hill, 12 and 13* **the unclean spirits begged him, "Send us to the pigs, so we can go into them."** **(Notice how the** **spirits transfer** **from one body to another)** *1 Yeshua gave them permission. They came out and entered the pigs; and the herd, numbering around two thousand, rushed down the hillside into the lake and were drowned. 14 The swineherds fled and told it in the town and in the surrounding country, and the people went to see what had happened. 15*

They came to Yeshua and saw the man who had had the legion of demons, sitting there, dressed and in his right mind; **(he was also possessed with a spirit of insanity)** *and they were frightened.*

Personal Study- Answer to Mark 1:32, 34
Spirits of infirmity (spirits that cause physical weakness) and unclean spirits 32 *That evening after sundown, they brought to Yeshua all* **who were ill or held in the power of demons, 33** *and the whole town came crowding around the door.* **34** *He healed many who were* **ill with various diseases and expelled many demons,** *but he did not allow the demons to speak, because they knew who he was.*

Personal Study- Answer to Luke 4:40-41
Spirits of infirmity, unclean spirits and familiar spirit 40 *After sunset, all those who had people* **sick with various diseases** *brought them to Yeshua, and he put his hands on each one of them and healed them;* **41** *also demons came out of many, crying,* **"You are the Son of God!" But, rebuking them, (Jesus would not allow the familiar spirit to speak)** *he did not permit them to say that* **they knew he was the Messiah**

A spirit of infirmity will cause physical weakness but there will be an outward manifestation of some kind or type of symptom ....I want us to look at Luke 13:10

Luke 13:10-13 (nkjv)
And behold, there was a woman who had a **spirit of infirmity eighteen years,** *and* **was bent over and could in no way raise herself up.** *12 But when Jesus saw her, He called her to Him and said to her, "Woman, you are loosed from your infirmity." 13 And He laid His hands on her, and* **immediately she was made straight,** *and glorified God*

Luke 13:10-11 (cjb)
A woman came up who had a **spirit which had crippled her for eighteen years;** *she was bent double and unable to stand erect at all. 12 On seeing her, Yeshua called her and said to her, "**Lady, you***

have been set free from your weakness!" 13 He put his hands on her, and at once she stood upright and began to glorify God.

Personal Study – Answer to - Matthew 9:32-34
Deaf and dumb spirit; (this word dumb in the Greek asthenia means to blunt or make speechless and deaf) unclean or evil spirit and a religious *spirit 32 as they were going, a man* **controlled by a demon** *and unable to speak was brought to Yeshua. 33 After the demon was expelled the man who had been mute spoke, and the crowds were amazed. "Nothing like this has ever been seen in Isra'el," they said. 34 But the* **P'rushim** *(Pharisees) said, "It is through the ruler of the demons that he expels demons."*

The Gifts of Healing It is the supernatural power given by God to remove diseases and the work of Satan in the human body. There is a difference between the gifts of healing and simply receiving healing by general faith in God's word. **Jesus operated in the Gifts of Healing-** Acts 10:38. **In our day, we have individuals like Kathryn Kuhlman, Benny Hinn and Oral Roberts all of whom had ministries that were or are known for the Gifts of Healing in manifestation.**

Let's compare the following two scriptures for scriptural support.

Luke 8:43-48
43 Now a woman, having a flow of blood for twelve years, who had spent all her livelihood on physicians and could not be healed by any, 44 came from behind and touched the border of His garment. And immediately her flow of blood stopped. 45 And Jesus said, **"Who touched Me**?" *When all denied it, Peter and those with him said, "Master, the multitudes throng and press You, and You say, 'Who touched Me?'* "46 But Jesus said, **"Somebody touched Me, for I perceived power going out from Me."** 47 Now when* **the woman saw that she was not hidden**, *she came trembling; and falling down before Him,* **she declared to Him in the presence of all the people the reason she had touched Him and how she was healed**

immediately. 48 And He said to her, "Daughter, be of good cheer; your faith has made you well. Go in peace."

Matthew 9: 20-22 *And suddenly, a **woman who had a flow of blood for twelve years** came from behind and touched the hem of His garment. 21 For she **said to herself, "If only I may touch His garment, I shall be made well."** 22 But Jesus turned around, and when He saw her He said, "Be of good cheer, daughter; **your faith has made you well."** And the woman was made well from that hour.*

It was this woman's "Faith" released by action that activated her healing.

Mark 10: 46-52

46 *Now they came to Jericho. As He went out of Jericho with His disciples and a great multitude, **blind Bartimaeus, the son of Timaeus, sat by the road begging. 47 And when he heard that it was Jesus of Nazareth, he began to cry out and say, "Jesus, Son of David, have mercy on me!"** 48 Then many warned him to be quiet; but he cried out all the more, "Son of David, have mercy on me!" 49 So Jesus stood still and commanded him to be called. **Then they called the blind man,** saying to him, "Be of good cheer. Rise, He is calling you." 50 **And throwing aside his garment, he rose and came to Jesus. 51 So Jesus answered and said to him, "What do you want Me to do for you?" The blind man said to Him, "Rabboni, that I may receive my sight." 52 Then Jesus said to him, "Go your way; your faith has made you well." And immediately he received his sight and followed Jesus on the road.***

Again it was this man's "Faith" released by his actions that activated his healing.

Old Testament

2 Kings 5 – This is the story of Naaman being healed of leprosy. We see the prophet Elisha healing Naaman of leprosy by flowing in the gifts of the Spirit, in **verse 10** his servant is to tell Naaman "go and wash in the Jordan seven times and your **flesh shall be restored** to you and you shall be clean" . Naaman, full of pride is reluctant to obey the instructions until his maid servant in *verse 13* puts him in check regarding his behavior. In *verse 14* he went down and dipped seven times in the Jordan, according to the saying of the man of God and his **flesh was restored like the flesh of a little child. (His disease was removed and his health restored.)**

Lesson 6

The Gift of Miracles

REVIEW ~ RUMINATE ~ REFLECT

<u>Acts 10:38</u>: *God anointed Jesus with the Holy Spirit and with power, who went about doing good and **healing all who were oppressed** by the devil, for God was with Him.*

<u>Gifts of the Holy Spirit 1 Corinthians 12:1- 11</u>

<u>There are nine spiritual gifts:</u> three **which are Spoken Gifts** - diverse tongues; interpretation of tongues and prophecy; **three which are Power Gifts** - healing; working of miracles; faith and **three which are Revelatory Gifts** – word of wisdom; word of knowledge; discerning of spirits.

- **The Word of Wisdom** is a supernatural revelation from God/Holy Spirit pointing to the future. It might be audible; visionary or given in a dream. It includes the mind, the will and purpose of God and should not be confused with man's natural wisdom found in **<u>James 3: 13-17.</u>**
- **The Word of Knowledge** is a supernatural revelation from God/Holy Spirit specifically pertaining to facts or events. The Word of Knowledge also gives revelation about things past or present, it is never revelation of the future. It can be manifested through a vision; given as spiritual enlightenment or inward revelation.
- **The Discerning of Spirits** is supernatural revelation or insight from God/Holy Spirit to identify activity in the realm of the spirit in situations or circumstances. Spiritual discernment is not reading the mind but rather identifying the activity that is promoted and or demonstrated by demonic spirits. This is not

101

a natural feeling or knowing. It is formulated in your spirit not in your soul (mind, will, emotions)

- **The Gift of Healing** is the supernatural power given by God/Holy Spirit to remove diseases and the work of Satan in the human body. There is a difference between the gifts of healing and simply receiving healing by general faith in God's word. Jesus operated in the Gifts of Healing- **Acts 10:38**. In our day, we have individuals like Kathryn Kuhlman, Benny Hinn and Oral Roberts had ministries that were/are known for the Gifts of Healing in manifestation.

Examples of Gift of Healing found in:
Luke 8:43-48

*43 Now a woman, having a flow of blood for twelve years, who had spent all her livelihood on physicians and could not be healed by any, 44 came from behind and touched the border of His garment. And immediately her flow of blood stopped. 45 And Jesus said, "**Who touched Me**?" When all denied it, Peter and those with him said, "Master, the multitudes throng and press You, and You say, 'Who touched Me?' "46 But Jesus said, "**Somebody touched Me, for I perceived power going out from Me.**" 47 Now when the woman saw that she was not hidden, she came trembling; and falling down before Him, she declared to Him in the presence of all the people the reason she had touched Him and how she was healed immediately. 48 And He said to her, "Daughter, be of good cheer; your faith has made you well. Go in peace."*

Matthew 9: 20-22

And suddenly, a woman who had a flow of blood for twelve years came from behind and touched the hem of His garment. 21 For she said to herself, "If only I may touch His garment, I shall be made well." 22 But Jesus turned around, and when He saw her He said, "Be of good cheer, daughter; your faith has made you well." And the woman was made well from that hour.

It was this woman's "Faith" released by her actions that activated her healing.

Mark 10: 46-52

*46 Now they came to Jericho. As He went out of Jericho with His disciples and a great multitude, **blind Bartimaeus, the son of Timaeus, sat by the road begging.** 47 **And when he heard that it was Jesus of Nazareth, he began to cry out and say, "Jesus, Son of David, have mercy on me!"** 48* Then many warned him to be quiet; but he cried out all the more, "Son of David, have mercy on me!" *49* So Jesus stood still and commanded him to be called. **Then they called the blind man,** saying to him, "Be of good cheer. Rise, He is calling you." **50 And throwing aside his garment, he rose and came to Jesus. 51 So Jesus answered and said to him, "What do you want Me to do for you?"** The blind man said to Him, "Rabboni, that I may receive my sight." **52 Then Jesus said to him, "Go your way; your faith has made you well."** And immediately he received his sight and followed Jesus on the road.*

Again it was this man's "Faith" released by his actions that activated his healing.

Old Testament

<u>2 Kings 5</u> *this is the story of Naaman being healed of leprosy. We see the prophet Elisha healing Naaman of leprosy by flowing in the gifts of the Spirit, in **verse 10**- his servant is to tell Naaman " go and wash in the Jordan seven times and your **flesh shall be restored** to you and you shall be clean" . He went down and dipped seven times in the Jordan, according to the saying of the man of God and his <u>**flesh was restored**</u> like the flesh of a little child.* **(His disease was removed and his health restored.)**

The Working of Miracles is a supernatural power given by God/Holy Spirit to alter the physical order of something of substance (physical matter) or something that is tangible which produces a sign and wonder. **Working of Miracles should not be confused with healings that occur miraculously**.

Let's look at some examples of miracles in the Old Testament:

2 Kings 6: 1-7 the floating ax head. Metal does not float, it sinks.

Exodus 7:19, 20 the water in Egypt was turned to blood by Moses using his rod to strike the waters.
19 ADONAI said to Moshe, "Say to Aharon, 'Take your staff, reach out your hand over the waters of Egypt, over their rivers, canals, ponds and all their reservoirs, so that they can turn into blood. There will be blood throughout the whole land of Egypt, even in the wooden buckets and stone jars.'" 20 Moshe and Aharon did exactly what ADONAI had ordered. He raised the staff and, in the sight of Pharaoh and his servants, struck the water in the river; and all the water in the river was turned into blood.

Exodus 8:20-23 the Lord sends swarms of flies over all of Egypt but not in the city called Goshen where His children are dwelling.

20 ADONAI said to Moshe, "Get up early in the morning, stand before Pharaoh when he goes out to the water and say to him, 'Here is what ADONAI says: "Let my people go, so that they can worship me. 21 Otherwise, if you won't let my people go, I will send swarms of insects on you, your servants and your people, and into your houses. The houses of the Egyptians will be full of swarms of insects, and likewise the ground they stand on. 22 But I will set apart the land of Goshen, where my people live - no swarms of insects will be there - so that you can realize that I am ADONAI, right here in the land. 23 Yes, I will distinguish between my people and your people, and this sign will happen by tomorrow."'" 24 ADONAI did it: terrible swarms of insects went into Pharaoh's palace and into all his servants 'houses - the insects ruined the entire land of Egypt.

Exodus 8:22-26 God orchestrated a hail storm mixed with fire to destroy crops, animals, people and vegetation that were left

exposed. Only in Goshen where his children were was their safety from the hail storm.

Personal Study: Read additional miracles wrought by the hand of God in **Exodus chapters 9, 10, 11, 14**

New Testament

John 6: 5-14 (cjb) Feeding the Multitude

Now the Judean festival of Pesach (Passover Festival) was coming up; 5 so when Yeshua looked up and saw that a large crowd was approaching, he said to Philip, "Where will we be able to buy bread, so that these people can eat?" 6 (Now Yeshua said this to test Philip, for Yeshua himself knew what he was about to do.) 7 Philip answered, "Half a year's wages wouldn't buy enough bread for them -- each one would get only a bite!" 8 One of the talmidim (disciples), Andrew the brother of Shim`on Kefa, said to him, 9 "There's a young fellow here who has five loaves of barley bread and two fish. But how far will they go among so many?" 10 Yeshua said, "Have the people sit down." There was a lot of grass there, so they sat down. The number of men was about five thousand. 11 Then Yeshua took the loaves of bread, and, after making a b'rakhah (prayer of thanksgiving), gave to all who were sitting there, and likewise with the fish, as much as they wanted. 12 After they had eaten their fill, he told his talmidim, "Gather the leftover pieces, so that nothing gets wasted." 13 They gathered them and filled twelve baskets with the pieces from the five barley loaves left by those who had eaten. 14 When the people saw the miracle he had performed, they said, "This has to be `the prophet' who is supposed to come into the world."

Luke 7:11-16 The Dead Raised

11 The next day Yeshua, accompanied by his talmidim and a large crowd, went to a town called Na`im. 12 As he approached the town gate, a dead man was being carried out for burial. His mother was a widow, this had been her only son, and a sizeable crowd from the town was with her. 13 When the Lord saw her, he felt com passion for her and said to her, "Don't cry." 14 Then he came close and touched the coffin, and the pallbearers halted. He said, "Young man, I say to you: get up!" **15** The dead man sat up and began to speak, and Yeshua gave him to his mother. **16 They were all filled with awe and gave glory to God, saying, "A great prophet has appeared among us," and, "God has come to help his people."**

Matthew 21:18-21 Withered Tree

18 *The next morning, on his way back to the city, he felt hungry.* **19** *Spotting a fig tree by the road, he went up to it but found nothing on it except leaves. So he said to it, "May you never again bear fruit!" and immediately the fig tree dried up.* **20** *The talmidim saw this and were amazed. "How did the fig tree dry up so quickly?" they asked.* **21** *Yeshua answered them, "Yes! I tell you, if you have trust and don't doubt, you will not only do what was done to this fig tree; but even if you say to this mountain, `Go and throw yourself into the sea!' it will be done.* **22 In other words, you will receive everything you ask for in prayer, no matter what it is, provided you have trust/faith." Evidence that miracles can be worked or wrought through our hands today.....Faith and trust in the Holy Spirit's ability to work through these jars of clay, hands of flesh must be evident.**

Acts 13:8-12 Elymas Temporary Blindness

8 *the sorcerer Elymas (for that is how his name is translated) opposed them, doing his best to turn the governor away from the faith.* **9** *Then Sha'ul, also known as Paul, filled with the Ruach HaKodesh, stared straight at him and said,* **10** *"You son of Satan, full of fraud and evil! You enemy of everything good! Won't you ever stop making crooked the straight paths of the Lord?* **11 So now, look! The hand of the Lord is upon you; and for a while you will be blind, unable to see the sun." Immediately mist and darkness came over Elymas; and he groped about, trying to find someone to lead him by the hand.**

Next lesson we will take a look at the Gift of Faith.

Personal Study Questions:

1. There are four kinds of Faith....can you list them?
2. Where are they located in scripture?

Lesson 7

The Gift of Faith

REVIEW ~ RUMINATE ~ REFLECT

<u>Acts 10:38</u> *God anointed Jesus with the Holy Spirit and with power, who went about doing good and* **healing all who were oppressed** *by the devil, for God was with Him.*

<u>Gifts of the Holy Spirit 1 Corinthians 12:1- 11</u>

<u>There are nine spiritual gifts:</u> **three which are Spoken Gifts**-diverse tongues; interpretation of tongues and prophecy; **three which are Power Gifts** - healing; working of miracles; faith and **three which are Revelatory Gifts**– word of wisdom; word of knowledge; discerning of spirits.

- **The Word of Wisdom** is a supernatural revelation from God/Holy Spirit pointing to the future. It could be audible; visionary or given in a dream. It includes the mind, the will and purpose of God and should not be confused with man's natural wisdom found in <u>**James 3: 13-17**</u>
- **The Word of Knowledge** is a supernatural revelation from God/Holy Spirit specifically pertaining to facts or events in the past or present. It is never revelation of the future. **These two gifts should never be associated with astrology or horoscope readings.**
- **The Discerning of Spirits** is supernatural revelation or insight from God/Holy Spirit to identify activity in the realm of the spirit in situations or circumstances. Spiritual discernment helps us identify the activity that is promoted, demonstrated or manifested by demonic spirits.
- **The Gift of Healing** it is the supernatural power given by God/Holy Spirit to remove diseases and the work of Satan in

the human body. **There is a difference between the gifts of healing and simply receiving healing by general faith in God's word. Jesus operated in the Gifts of Healing** see Acts 10:38.

- **The Working of Miracles** is a supernatural power given by God/Holy Spirit to alter the physical order of tangible substance (physical matter) which produces a sign and/or a wonder. **Working of miracles should not be confused with healings that occur miraculously. The working of miracles works a miracle and the Gift of Faith receives a miracle.**

Present day ministries that have operated in the supernatural gift of healings and supernatural gift of miracles have been through individuals like Kathryn Kuhlman, Benny Hinn and Oral Roberts; all of which have been well documented and substantiated.

The Gift of Faith

To understand the **Gift of Faith** we have to understand that there are four categories of Faith:
1. General Faith
2. Saving Faith
3. Fruit of Faith
4. Gift of Faith

- *General Faith*   Everyone operates in general faith. If faith is the substance of things hoped for and the evidence of things not seen, then believers and unbelievers alike use their faith every day.

Example of General Faith   There are a number of things we can site but let's use technology. We believe that by using a cellphone, the satellite technology associated with cell towers will connect us to whomever we call digitally. We don't see the energy or the power source involved but because we believe in the technology we use the cellphone.

<u>Romans 12:3</u> states that God has given to every man a *measure of Faith.* General faith then is being persuaded by, placing confidence in or yielding or surrendering to something you believe in. This is your belief.

- *Saving Faith* a belief in Jesus Christ's gospel that leads one to salvation. Let's support this by the word of God.

<u>Romans 10: 8-13</u> **(cjb)** *What, then, does the bible say? "The word is near you,* **in other words the word of faith** *is in your mouth and in your heart. That is, the word about trust or faith which we proclaim,* **9** *that if you acknowledge publicly with your mouth that Yeshua is Lord and trust* **or have faith** *in your heart that God raised him from the dead, you will be delivered or saved.* **10** *For with the heart one goes on trusting or believing and thus continues toward righteousness, while with the mouth one keeps on making public acknowledgement and thus continues toward deliverance or salvation.* **11** *For the passage quoted says that everyone who rests his trust (or has faith) on him will not be humiliated.* **12** *That means that there is no difference between Jew and Gentile - ADONAI is the same for everyone, rich toward everyone who calls on him,* **13** *since everyone who calls on the name of ADONAI will be delivered or saved.*

<u>Ephesian 2:8</u> *For by grace are you saved through faith; and that not of yourselves; it is the gift of God......*

- **The Fruit of Faith** After one is born again there should be evidence or an outward manifestation of the recreated human spirit or the inward work that transformed ones old nature to a new nature. This manifestation is called the **"fruit of faith".** The new believer uses his or her faith to produce the inward fruit of the Holy Spirit in their lives on a consistent basis.

<u>Galatians 5:22-25</u> *But the fruit of the Spirit is love, joy, peace, patience, kindness, goodness, faithfulness,* **23** *humility, self-control. Nothing in the Torah stands against such things.* **24** *Moreover, those who belong to the Messiah Yeshua have put their old nature to death on the stake, along with*

its passions and desires. 25 Since it is through the Spirit that we have Life, let it also be through the Spirit that we order our lives day by day.

- **The Gift of Faith is** a supernatural power given by God/Holy Spirit to *receive miracles* and to *protect the believer*. Sometimes it is referred to as *"special faith"* and should not be confused with general or saving faith.

Let's start in the Old Testament to see what this kind of Faith looks like.

1 Kings 17: 10-15 (cjb)

On reaching the gate of the city, Elijah saw a widow gathering sticks. He called out to her, "Please bring a little water in a container for me to drink." 11 As she was going to get it, he called after her, "Please bring me a piece of bread in your hand." 12 She answered, "As ADONAI your God lives, I have nothing baked, only a handful of meal in a pot and a little oil in the jug. Here I am, gathering a couple sticks of wood, so that I can go and cook it for myself and my son. After we have eaten that, we will die." 13 Eliyahu said to her, "Don't be afraid. Go; and do what you said; but first, use a little of it to make me a small loaf of bread; and bring it out to me. After that, make food for yourself and your son. 14 For this is what ADONAI the God of Isra'el, says: 'The pot of meal will not get used up, nor will there fail to be oil in the jug, until the day ADONAI sends rain down on the land." 15 She went and acted according to what Eliyahu had said; and she, Elijah and her household had food to eat for a long time.

Let's see her transition from **general faith** to the **gift of faith**. Initially she was operating in general faith when she was looking for firewood to prepare for her last meal. She believed that she was about to make her last meal based upon what she had in her possession, a little meal in her barrel and a little oil in her cruse. Something happens when she listens to the words of the prophet. First of all Elijah asked her for some water, which she could give him, but then he asked for her to bring some bread along with the water. **The widow woman has to**

position herself to receive a miracle. She must act on the words of Elijah, the prophet without evidence that his word to her will come to pass. When she obeys the instructions she moves from general faith to a supernatural ability to believe, we see the gift of faith in operation. She had to believe that somehow by making bread for Elijah first would produce food for her and her household. She took him for his word and by acting on the word of the prophet she received the miracle of a multiplied harvest on her seed of oil and the meal/grain that would last until the famine was over. The gift of faith that she operated in was contrary to the laws of nature. She had to believe God and believe in the prophet that God sent.

<u>Daniel 6:</u> Tells a story of Daniel being thrown into a lion's den. Daniel operated with an excellent spirit which caused jealousy among King Darius's own elected officials. The King had decided to promote Daniel over them. This gave them great cause to find fault with Daniel that would strip him of his authority over them. Since they knew Daniel did not serve their gods, they influenced King Darius to write and sign a decree that would forbid anyone from praying to any other gods for 30 days.

In verse 10 (cjb) says: On learning that the document had been signed, Dani'el went home. The windows of his upstairs room were open in the direction of Yerushalayim; and there he kneeled down three times a day and prayed, giving thanks before his God, just as he had been doing before. 11 Then these men descended on Dani'el and found him making requests and pleading before his God.

(Daniel is demonstrating the gift of faith. He positions himself to receive a miracle and for protection against the punishment for praying to his God and not to King Darius's gods.)

12 So they remind the king of his royal decree: "Didn't you sign a law prohibiting anyone from making requests of any god or man within thirty days, except yourself, your majesty, on pain of being thrown into the lion pit?" 13 They replied to the king, "That Dani'el, one of the exiles from

Y'hudah, respects neither you, your majesty, nor the decree you signed; instead, he continues praying three times a

14 When the king heard this report, he was very upset. He determined to save Dani'el and worked until sunset to find a way to rescue him. 15 But these men descended on the king and said to him, "Remember, your majesty, **that no decree or edict, once issued by the king, can be revoked." 16** *So the king gave the order, and they brought Dani'el and threw him into the lion pit. The king said to Dani'el, "Your God, whom you are always serving, will save you."*

(King Darius is using general faith. He believes in the ability of Daniel's God to deliver Daniel and makes a statement of his faith).

17 A stone was brought to block the opening of the pit, the king sealed it with his own signet and with the signet of his lords, so that nothing concerning Dani'el could be changed. 18 Then the king returned to his palace. He spent the night fasting and refusing to be entertained, as sleep eluded him. 19 Early in the morning, the king got up and hurried to the lion pit. 20 On approaching the pit where Dani'el was, the king cried in a pained voice to Dani'el, "Dani'el, servant of the living God! Has your God, whom you are always serving, been able to save you from the lions?" 21 Then Dani'el answered the king, "May the king live forever! 22 My God sent his angel to shut the lions' mouths, so they haven't hurt me. This is because before him I was found innocent; and also I have done no harm to you, your majesty." 23 The king was overjoyed and ordered Dani'el taken up from the pit. So Dani'el was taken up from the pit, and he was found to be completely unharmed, because he had trusted in his God. 24 Then the king gave an order, and they brought those men who had accused Dani'el, and they threw them into the lion pit - them, their children and their wives -and before they even reached the bottom of the pit, the lions had them in their control and broke all their bones to pieces. 25 King Daryavesh wrote all the peoples, nations and languages living anywhere on earth: "Shalom rav! (Abundant peace)! 26 "I herewith issue a decree that everywhere in my kingdom, people are to tremble and be in awe of the God of Dani'el."For he is the living God; he endures forever. His kingdom will never be destroyed; his rulership will last till the end. 27 He saves, rescues, does signs and wonders both in heaven and on earth. He delivered Dani'el from the power of the lions." 28 So this Dani'el prospered.....

Lesson 8

Four Kinds of Faith

REVIEW ~ RUMINATE ~ REFLECT

<u>Acts 10:38</u> *God anointed Jesus with the Holy Spirit and with power, who went about doing good and **healing all who were oppressed** by the devil, for God was with Him.*

<u>Gifts of the Holy Spirit 1 Corinthians 12:1- 11</u>

<u>There are nine spiritual gifts;</u> three which are **Spoken Gifts**-diverse tongues; interpretation of tongues and prophecy; **three which are Power Gifts** - healing; working of miracles; faith **and three which are Revelatory Gifts** – word of wisdom; word of knowledge; discerning of spirits

- **The Word of Wisdom** is a supernatural revelation from God/Holy Spirit pointing to the future. It could be audible; visionary or given in a dream. It includes the mind, the will and purpose of God and should not be confused with man's natural wisdom found in <u>James 3: 13-17</u>.
- **The Word of Knowledge** is a supernatural revelation from God/Holy Spirit specifically pertaining to facts or events in the past or present. It is never revelation of the future. **These two gifts should never be associated with astrology or horoscope readings.**
- **The Discerning of Spirits** is supernatural revelation or insight from God/Holy Spirit to identify demonic activity in the realm of the spirit in situations or circumstances. Spiritual discernment helps us identify the activity that is promoted, demonstrated or manifested by demonic spirits.
- **The Gift of Healing** is the supernatural power given by God/Holy Spirit to remove diseases and the work of Satan in

the human body. There is a difference between the gift of healing and simply receiving healing by general faith in God's word. Jesus operated in the Gift of Healing see **Acts 10:38.**

- **The Working of Miracles is** a supernatural power given by God/Holy Spirit to alter the physical order of tangible substance (physical matter) which produces a sign and/or a wonder. **Working of Miracles should not be confused with healings that occur miraculously.** The Working of Miracles works a miracle and the Gift of Faith receives a miracle.

- **The Gift of Faith** is a supernatural power given by God/Holy Spirit to receive miracles and/or to protect the believer. Sometimes it is referred to as **"special faith"** and should not be confused with general or saving faith.

There are four different kinds of Faith

1. General Faith Everyone operates in general faith. If Faith is the substance of things hoped for and the evidence of things not seen, then believers and unbelievers alike use their faith every day. **Romans 12:3** states that God has given to every man a *measure of Faith.*

2. Saving Faith a belief in Jesus Christ's gospel that leads one to salvation. **Romans 10:8-13 and Ephesians 2:8**

3. Fruit of Faith After one is born again there should evidence or an outward manifestation of the recreated human spirit or the inward work that transformed one old nature to a new nature. This manifestation is called the **"fruit of faith"**. The new believer uses his/her faith to produce the inward fruit of the Holy Spirit in their lives on a consistent basis. **Galatians 5:22-25**

4. Gift of Faith is a supernatural power given by God/Holy Spirit to **receive miracles** and to **protect the believer**.

<u>1 Kings 17: 10-15</u> - the widow woman transitioned from general faith to gift of faith by acting upon what she was instructed to do without any evidence the word would come to pass.

<u>Daniel 6 -</u> Daniel used the gift of faith when he positioned himself to receive a miracle and protection against being thrown into the lion's den for praying to his God and not to King Darius's gods.
King Darius on the other hand used general faith when he verbalized his belief in Daniel's God's ability to deliver Daniel from the lions.

Thus far we have talked about 6 of the 9 gifts of the Spirit. I want us to look at a passage of scripture that will allow us to see how many of the gifts can work together in one person to bring glory to God and demonstrate signs and wonders to the unbelieving.

<u>John 11:1-44</u>
Verse 1 Lazarus is sick.
Verse 3 Mary and Martha the sisters of Lazarus sent for Jesus and said Lord, behold he whom You love is *sick.*
Verse 4 When Jesus heard that He speaks by a **Word of Wisdom (future being revealed)** saying, *"This sickness is not unto death, but for the glory of God that the Son of God may be glorified through it"*
Verse 6 When Jesus heard that he was sick, Jesus remains where He is for two more days. **The Gift of Faith is in manifestation (Jesus was in position to receive the miracle).**

Prophetic Word - I heard the Lord clearly say that **when we hear** Faith should come .....**when you hear** that you are sick, **when you hear** you don't have enough money, **when you hear** that you will lose your job....**whatever we hear**......Faith should come! The Holy Spirit will manifest and His gifts will operate..... **Resist the temptation to Fear!**

Verse 7 they prepare to go to Judea

Verses 11, 14 *Jesus says "our friend Lazarus sleeps but I go that I may wake him up"- Lazarus is not sleeping but dead, Jesus was speaking* by **The Word of Knowledge (present event or fact is revealed)**

*Verse 34- 44 And He said, "Where have you laid him?" They said to Him, "Lord, come and see." 35 **Jesus wept. (He was emotional)** 36 Then the Jews said, "**See how He loved him!**"***(His compassion was on display)*** 37 and some of them said, "**Could not this Man, who opened the eyes of the blind, also have kept this man from dying?**"*

They are speaking about Jesus' humanity not his deity. The gifts of the Holy Spirit are operating through a Man! **Verse 39** *the stone is removed and Martha says "Lord by this time there is a stench for he has been dead four days.* **Verse 42, 43** *He gives thanks to God for the* "**The Working of Miracle**" which is about to take place for the benefit of those that are present. Jesus had to call Lazarus by name, so others who were dead would not come forth. **Verse 44** *He who had died came out bound hand and foot with grave clothes, and his face was wrapped with a cloth, Jesus said to them* **"loose him and let him go".**

John 12: 1-2, 9-11

Then, six days before the Passover, Jesus came to Bethany, where Lazarus was who had been dead, whom He had raised from the dead. 2 There they made Him a supper; and Martha served, but Lazarus was one of those who sat at the table with Him. 9 Now a great many of the Jews knew that He was there; and they came, not for Jesus' sake only, but that they might also see Lazarus, whom He had raised from the dead. 10 But the chief priests plotted to put Lazarus to death also, 11 because on account of him many of the Jews went away and believed in Jesus.

When raising Lazarus from the dead three gifts worked simultaneously.

The Gift of Faith **to call his spirit back into his dead body.**

The Working of Miracle **to raise Lazarus up.**

The Gift of Healing **to keep Lazarus from dying again.**

This scripture gives us a clear picture of just how many gifts of the Holy Spirit can be in operation at one time. There were five gifts flowing through Jesus (word of wisdom, gift of faith, word of knowledge, working of miracle, gift of healing) to bring about a sign and wonder to the unbelieving Jews and Pharisees. Some of the Jewish people were converted after being a witness to this great miracle.

Let's talk about **Prophecy.**

Prophecy is a supernatural utterance inspired by God in a known language.

1 Corinthians 14 (cjb)

1 *Pursue love! However, keep on eagerly seeking the things of the Spirit; and* ***especially seek to be able to prophesy.*** *In other words to have inspiring messages that come from God.* **2** *For someone speaking in a tongue is not speaking to people but to God, because no one can understand, since he is uttering mysteries in the power of the Spirit.* **3** ***But someone prophesying is speaking to people, edifying, encouraging and comforting them.*** **4** *A person speaking in a tongue does edify himself, but a person prophesying edifies the congregation.* **5** ***I wish you would all speak in tongues, but even more I wish you would all prophesy. The person who prophesies is greater than the person who speaks in tongues, unless someone gives an interpretation, so that the congregation can be edified.***

Paul is addressing all believers in the church in this chapter......those who seek spiritual gifts and those who speak under the inspiration of the Holy Spirit. The gift of prophecy comes by inspiration and is for anyone that desires the gift. **Prophecy should not be confused with the Prophet's ministry or one who stands in the office of the Prophet which is a fivefold ministry gift.** A Prophet's ministry usually demonstrate several gifts of the Holy Spirit on a consistent basis like we saw Jesus exhibited.

Let's look at some examples of the simple gift of prophecy:

Ezekiel 37

Ezekiel is a Priest and a Prophet or stands in the office of Pastor/Prophet. He delivers God's messages by using prophecy, signs and parables to minister to those to whom he was sent.

*1 With the hand of ADONAI upon me, ADONAI carried me out by his Spirit and set me down in the middle of the valley, and it was full of bones. 2 He had me pass by all around them - there were so many bones lying in the valley, and they were so dry! 3 He asked me, "**Human being, can these bones live?" I answered, "Adonai ELOHIM! Only you know that!"** 4 Then he said to me, "**Prophesy over these bones! Say to them, 'Dry bones! Hear what ADONAI has to say!** 5 To these bones Adonai ELOHIM says, "I will make breath enter you, and you will live. 6 I will attach ligaments to you, make flesh grow on you, cover you with skin and put breath in you. You will live, and you will know that I am ADONAI." 7 So I prophesied as ordered; and while I was prophesying, there was a noise, a rattling sound; it was the bones coming together, each bone in its proper place. 8 As I watched, ligaments grew on them, flesh appeared and skin covered them; but there was no breath in them. 9 Next he said to me, "Prophesy to the breath! Prophesy, human being! Say to the breath that Adonai ELOHIM says, 'Come from the four winds, breath; and breathe on these slain, so that they can live." 10 So I prophesied as ordered, and the* *breath came into them, and they were alive! They stood up on their feet, a huge army! 11 Then he said to me, "Human being! These bones are the whole house of Isra'el; and they are saying, 'Our bones have dried up, our hope is gone, and we are completely cut off.' 12 Therefore prophesy; say to them that Adonai ELOHIM says, 'My people! I will open your graves and make you get up out of your graves, and I will bring you into the land of Isra'el. 13 Then you will know that I am ADONAI - when I have opened your graves and made you get up out of your graves, my people! 14 I will put my Spirit in you; and you will be alive. Then I will place you in your own land; and you will know that I, ADONAI, have spoken, and that I have done it,' says ADONAI."*

This prophecy pertains to the house of Israel's future. They are dead but will be brought back alive. They will take possession of their land which symbolically is the kingdom of God.

Lesson 9

The Gift of Prophecy

REVIEW ~ RUMINATE ~ REFLECT

<u>Acts 10:38</u> *God anointed Jesus with the Holy Spirit and with power, who went about doing good and <u>healing all who were oppressed</u> by the devil, for God was with Him.*

<u>**Gifts of the Holy Spirit 1 Corinthians 12:1- 11**</u>

<u>**There are nine spiritual gifts:**</u> **three which are Spoken Gifts** -diverse tongues; interpretation of tongues and prophecy; **three which are Power Gifts** - healing; working of miracles; faith and **three which are Revelatory Gifts** – word of wisdom; word of knowledge; discerning of spirits.

The Word of Wisdom is a supernatural revelation from God/Holy Spirit pointing to the future. It could be audible; visionary or given in a dream.

The Word of Knowledge is a supernatural revelation from God/Holy Spirit specifically pertaining to facts or events in the past or present.

The Discerning of Spirits is supernatural revelation or insight from God/Holy Spirit to identify demonic activity in the realm of the spirit in situations or circumstances.

The Gift of Healing is the supernatural power given by God/Holy Spirit to remove diseases and the work of Satan in the human body.

The Working of Miracles is a supernatural power given by God/Holy Spirit to alter the physical order of tangible substance (physical matter) which produces a sign and/or a wonder.

The Gift of Faith is a supernatural power given by God/Holy Spirit to **receive miracles** and/or to **protect the believer**.

Spiritual Gifts can work simultaneously together – like in John 11- the story of Lazarus. He received a miracle by being raised from the dead.

The Gift of Faith manifested to call the spirit and soul back into the body.

The Working of Miracle raised the body up or bring life (much like what happened when Jesus was raised from the dead.) Romans 8:10, 11. The Holy Spirit who is the Giver of the gifts also breathed life and quickened the mortal body of Jesus to raise it up.

The Gift of Healing was needed to keep the body from dying again.

Let's now turn our attention to the Gift of Prophecy.

The Gift of Prophecy *is* **a supernatural utterance inspired by God in a known language.**

What should we know about prophecy in 1 Corinthians 14? (cjb)

1. Especially seek to be able to prophesy.

2. Prophecy should edify, encourage and comfort. (makes you feel good about yourself or your circumstances)

3. The person who prophesies is greater than the person who speaks in tongues, unless someone gives an interpretation, so that all of the congregation is edified.

4. Paul says those who seek spiritual gifts should do so for the edification of the church.

5. The gift of prophecy comes by inspiration of the Holy Spirit and is for anyone that desires the gift.

6. Prophecy when heard by an unbeliever will bring conviction. Verse **24, 25**-says *But if all prophecy and an unbeliever or uninformed person is present, he is convinced by those speaking and convicted by all present, and thus the secrets of his heart are revealed and so falling down on his face he will worship God and report that God is truly present.*

7. Prophecy should always follow the protocol of the public setting or protocol of the church or assembly.

8. Prophets or spiritual leaders should judge the words spoken through prophecy.

Everyone can prophesy but not everyone is a prophet or set apart to function in the office of a prophet. (**Ephesians 4:11**) Prophecy should always be edifying, encouraging and comforting.

A Prophet usually speaks prophetically to give instructions, bring correction and reveal pending judgement and he usually addresses sin which is willful disobedience; iniquity which is moral wickedness and transgressions which refers to using poor judgement. An excellent example of this is when Nathan, the Prophet confronts David regarding the death of Uriah and sin with Bathsheba. A true prophet addresses sin. Like a surgeon, they will go to the root causes, remove it, stitch you up and put healing salve on you to help you heal and stay healed and whole!

<u>**2 Peter 1:19-21**</u> **(cjb)** *Yes, we have the prophetic Word made very certain. You will do well to pay attention to it as to a light shining in a dark, murky place, until the Day dawns and the Morning Star rises in your hearts.* **20** *First of all, understand this: no prophecy of Scripture is to be interpreted by an individual on his own;* **21** *for never has a prophecy come as a result of human willing - on the contrary, people moved by the Ruach HaKodesh*

spoke a message from God. **In other words, the bible is the sure Word of prophecy, it has been documented as the inspired Word of God with prophetic words that have been fulfilled and some that are yet to be fulfilled. The revelation that comes from the Word comes from the Holy Spirit, Ruach HaKodesh and is revealed to those who He appoints.**

Let's look at more examples …….

Joel 2:28 **Joel was a prophet to Judah, his calling was to a prophetic office, speaking prophetically regarding the end times giving instruction and speaking of pending judgements.** *Verse 28, says "After this, (after the restoration of God's people Israel) God will pour out His Spirit on all humanity.* **Your sons and daughters will prophesy,** *your old men will dream dreams, your young men will see visions;*

Acts 3:14-18 Peter's sermon on the day of Pentecost, after all present had received the baptism of the Holy Spirit. Joel's prophecy was fulfilled that day!

Acts 21:8, 9 The following day, we left and came to Caesarea, where we went to the home of Philip the Evangelist a proclaimer of the Good News and one of the seven, and stayed with him. **9 He had four unmarried daughters with the gift of prophecy. Woman prophesying!**

Samuel the prophet speaking to King Saul

1 Samuel 10:5, 6, 10 *After that, you will come to Giv'ah (hill) of God, where the P'lishtim (philistines) are garrisoned. On arrival at the city there, you will meet a group of prophets coming down from the high place, preceded by lutes, tambourines, flutes and lyres; and they will be prophesying. 6 Then the Spirit of ADONAI will fall on you; you will prophesy with them and be turned into another man! 10 When they arrived at the hill, and there in front of him was a group of prophets, the Spirit of God fell on him and he prophesied along with them. 11 When those who knew him from before saw him there,* *prophesying with the prophets, they asked each other, "What's happened to Kish's son? **Is Sha'ul a prophet, too?" 12** Someone in the crowd answered, "Must prophets' fathers be special?" So it became an expression "Is Sha'ul a prophet, too?" **13** When he had finished prophesying, he arrived at the high place.*

Saul was not a prophet but a king who when the Holy Spirit came upon him he prophesied....the gift of prophecy.

Saul's soldiers 1 <u>Samuel 19:20</u> *Sha'ul sent messengers to capture David. But when they saw the group of prophets prophesying, with Sh'mu'el standing and leading them, **the Spirit of God fell on Sha'ul's messengers; and they <u>too began prophesying</u>**.*

How to identify a true Prophet

<u>Old Testament</u>
1. Prophets were divine philosophers, instructors and guides of the Hebrews.
2. They were also called Seers (one who perceives mentally the purpose of God) **<u>1 Samuel 9.</u>**
3. Sometimes they were called **"chozeh"** meaning a beholder, one who has visions or supernatural revelations.
4. They generally lived retired lives and only made public appearances when they had to deliver a message from God to the people.
5. Sons of the prophets were students trained by the older prophets in religious piety and devotion. These were theology students studying the law and history.

6. There were several schools of the prophet....remember Elijah was a head-master over schools in Gilgal, Bethel and Jericho **(<u>1 Kings 12, 13, 20</u>)**. The fruit of the anointing of God should be evident upon their lives and their ministries. **<u>1 Kings 19, Isaiah 61:1, 2, Acts 3:21</u>**
7. The bible lists *78 Prophets*

8. The bible lists and records *14* **Prophetesses. The Hebrew word describes them as "Hannebiah" or prophetesses** and they are as follows:

- Rachel **Genesis 30:24**; (Rachel predicted that God would add to her another son, also an example of one prophesying over oneself)
- **Miriam** Exodus 15:20;
- **Huldah**- 2 Kings 22:14, 2 Chronicles 34:22;
- **Noadiah**- Nehemiah 6:14;
- **Isaiah's wife**- Isaiah 8:3;
- **Deborah**- Judges 4:4;
- **Elizabeth**- Luke 1:41-45;
- **Mary, mother of Jesus**- Luke 1:46-55;
- **Anna**- Luke 2:36-38;
- **Jezebel- false prophetess**- Revelation 2:20;
- **Philip's four daughters**- Acts 21:9

Deuteronomy 18:18-22 (cjb) *I will raise up for them a prophet like you (like Moses) from among their kinsmen.* **I will put my words in his mouth, and he will tell them everything I order him.** *19 Whoever doesn't listen to my words, which he will speak in my name, will have to account for himself to me. 20 "'But if a prophet presumptuously speaks a word in my name which I didn't order him to say, or if he speaks in the name of other gods, then that prophet must die.' 21 You may be wondering, 'How are we to know if a word has not been spoken by ADONAI?'22 When a prophet speaks in the name of ADONAI, and the prediction does not come true -that is, the word is not fulfilled -then ADONAI did not speak that word. The prophet who said it spoke presumptuously; you have nothing to fear from him.*

This scripture is repeated in **Acts 3:20-25**- but let's turn our attention to **verse 24** which states that "yes and all the prophets from Samuel and those who follow, as many as have spoken, have also foretold these days.

In other words, prophets were and are necessary in the New Testament church as they were in the Old Testament. There must be a prophetic voice in the Church!

<u>Acts 11:27, 28</u> *And in these days came prophets from Jerusalem unto Antioch. And there stood up one called Agabus and signified by the spirit that there should be a great dearth throughout all the world **which came to pass in the days** of Claudius Cesar.*

<u>Acts 15:32</u> Prophets Judas and Silas were exhorting and strengthening the church with their preaching.

False Prophets

<u>Jeremiah 23:11-32-</u> *"Both prophet and cohen are godless; In my own house I find their wickedness," says ADONAI. 12 "Therefore their way will be slippery for them; they will be driven into darkness and fall there. For I will bring disaster upon them, their year of punishment," says ADONAI. 13 "I have seen inappropriate conduct in the prophets of Shomron - they prophesied by Ba'al and led my people Isra'el astray. 14 But in the prophets of Yerushalayim I have seen a horrible thing - they commit adultery, live in lies, so encouraging evildoers that none returns from his sin. For me they have all become like S'dom, its inhabitants like 'Amora. 15 Therefore, this is what ADONAI-Tzva'ot says concerning the prophets: "I will feed them bitter wormwood and make them drink poisonous water, for ungodliness has spread through all the land from the prophets of Yerushalayim." 16 ADONAI-Tzva'ot says: "Don't listen to the words of the prophets who are prophesying to you. They are making you act foolishly, telling you visions from their own minds and not from the mouth of ADONAI. 17 They keep reassuring those who despise me, 'ADONAI says you will be safe and secure,' and saying to all living by their own stubborn hearts, 'Nothing bad will happen to you.' 18 But which of them has been present at the* council

of ADONAI to see and hear his word? Who has paid attention to his word enough to hear it?" *22 If they have been present at my council, they should let my people hear my words and turn them from their evil way and the evil of their actions. 23 Am I God only when near," asks ADONAI, "and not when far away? 24 Can anyone hide in a place so secret that I won't see him?" asks ADONAI. ADONAI says, "Do I not fill heaven and earth? 25 "I have heard what these prophets prophesying lies in my name are saying: 'I've had a dream! I've had a dream!' 26 How long will this go on? Is [my word] in the hearts of prophets who are prophesying lies, who are prophesying the deceit of their own minds? 27 With their dreams that they keep telling each other, they hope to cause my people to forget my name; just as their ancestors forgot my name when they worshipped Ba'al. 28 "If a prophet has a dream, let him tell it as a dream. But someone who has my word should speak my word faithfully. What do chaff and wheat have in common?" asks ADONAI. 29 "Isn't my word like fire," asks ADONAI, "like a hammer shattering rocks? 30 So, I am against the prophets," says ADONAI, "who steal my words from each other. 31 Yes, I am against the prophets," says ADONAI, "who speak their own words, then add, 'He says.' 32 "I am against those who concoct prophecies out of fake dreams," says ADONAI. "They tell them, and by their lies and arrogance they lead my people astray. I didn't send them, I didn't commission them, and they don't do this people any good at all," says ADONAI.*

Jeremiah 14:14   *And the Lord said to me, "The prophets prophesy lies in My name. I have not sent them, commanded them, nor spoken to them; they prophesy to you a false vision, divination, a worthless thing, and the deceit of their heart.*
Lamentations 2:14   *Your prophets have seen for you False and deceptive visions; They have not uncovered your iniquity, (confront sin and bring you to conviction) To bring back your captives, But have envisioned for you false prophecies and delusions.*

Ezekiel 22:28 *Her prophets plastered them with untempered mortar, seeing false visions, and divining lies for them, saying, 'Thus says the Lord God,' when the Lord had not spoken.*

1 John 4: 1-3 *Dear friends, don't trust every spirit. On the contrary, test the spirits to see whether they are from God; because many false prophets have gone out into the world. 2 Here is how you recognize the Spirit of God: every spirit which acknowledges that Yeshua the Messiah came as a human being is from God, 3 and every spirit which does not acknowledge Yeshua is not from God - in fact, this is the spirit of the Anti-Messiah. You have heard that he is coming. Well, he's here now, in the world already!*

We are warned not to disrespect the anointing upon God's Prophets. **1 Chronicles 16:22; Psalms 105:15**

We are admonished to believe God's Prophets so we may prosper. **2 Chronicles 18:5**

God will deal with His prophets as we see history outlined in scripture. Our job is to discern the true prophet from the false prophet!

Lesson 10

The Gift of Tongues – Interpretation of Tongues

REVIEW ~ RUMINATE ~ REFLECT

<u>Acts 10:38</u> *God anointed Jesus with the Holy Spirit and with power, who went about doing good and* **healing all who were oppressed** *by the devil, for God was with Him.*

<u>Gifts of the Holy Spirit -1 Corinthians 12:1- 11</u>

<u>There are nine spiritual gifts:</u> **three which are Spoken Gifts** -diverse tongues; interpretation of tongues and prophecy; **three which are Power Gifts** - healing; working of miracles; faith and **three which are Revelatory** – word of wisdom; word of knowledge; discerning of spirits.

The Word of Wisdom is a supernatural revelation from God/Holy Spirit pointing to the future. It could be audible; visionary or given in a dream.

The Word of Knowledge is a supernatural revelation from God/Holy Spirit specifically pertaining to facts or events in the past or present.

The Discerning of Spirits is supernatural revelation or insight from God/Holy Spirit to identify demonic activity in the realm of the spirit in situations or circumstances.

The Gift of Healing is the supernatural power given by God/Holy Spirit to remove diseases and the work of Satan in the human body.

The Working of Miracles is a supernatural power given by God/Holy Spirit to alter the physical order of tangible substance (physical matter) which produces a sign and or a wonder.

The Gift of Faith is a supernatural power given by God/Holy Spirit to **receive miracles** and or to **protect the believer**.

The Gift of Prophecy is a supernatural utterance inspired by God in an unknown language.

It is possible then, when ministering you will experience situations where your spiritual gifts will operate simultaneously – like in John 11 (Lazarus being raised from the dead); 2 Kings 5 (Elisha's servant Gehazi's exposure of greed.

What should we know about T*he Gift of Prophecy* according to **1 Corinthians 14?**

1. We are to especially seek the gift of prophecy.
2. Prophecy should edify, encourage and comfort. (Makes us feel good about ourselves or our circumstances).
3. The person who prophesies is greater than the person who speaks in tongues, unless someone gives an interpretation, so that those who hear the message in tongues can be edified.
4. Paul says our only purpose to seek spiritual gifts should be for the edification of the church body.
5. The gift of prophecy comes by inspiration of the Holy Spirit and is for anyone who desires the gift.
6. Prophecy when heard by an unbeliever will bring conviction. Verse 24, 25-says if all prophecy and an unbeliever or uninformed person is present, he is convinced by those speaking and convicted by all present, and thus the secrets of his heart are revealed and so falling down on his face he will worship God and report that God is truly present.
7. Prophecy should always follow the protocol of the public setting protocol of the church or assembly.
8. Prophets or spiritual leaders should judge the words spoken through prophecy.

Everyone can prophesy but not everyone is a prophet or set apart to function in the office of a prophet. (Ephesians 4:11- fivefold ministry)   1 Samuel 19:20 – simple gift of prophesying displayed by Saul and his soldiers)

A Prophet usually speaks prophetically to give instructions; bring correction and reveal pending judgement. **He will also address sin, which is willful disobedience; iniquity which is moral wickedness and transgressions which refers to using poor judgement.**
An excellent example of this is found in **2 Samuel 12: 1-15** when Nathan, the Prophet confronts David regarding the death of Uriah and the sin of adultery with Bathsheba.
A true prophet addresses sin in order to bring judgement and healing. Think of it like this. In the natural sense a surgeon will address the root cause of a disease that is disrupting the healthy function of the body. Through a surgical procedure he then removes the cause; closes the wound with sutures in order to bind the wound and puts healing salve on the wound to help you heal and make you whole! That is what Nathan accomplished with David. David confessed his sin and was cleansed and made whole. Psalm 51. More importantly, Jesus would still be able to come through the seed of David for the total healing of God's people that includes you and I.

- **Sin-** willful or deliberate act or violation of the law.
- **Iniquity-** gross injustice or moral wickedness which is perpetuated from generation to generation.
- **Transgression-** to step across the line using poor judgement.

These are moral failures of varying degrees. David's **transgression** was poor judgement in watching Bathsheba bath; then moved to **sin** because he deliberately arranged for Uriah's death; then gross injustice turned into **iniquity** which was passed on to his son Absalom.

2 Peter 1:19-21- the bible is the sure Word of prophecy, it has been documented as the inspired Word of God with prophetic words that have been fulfilled and some that are yet to be fulfilled.

The Gift of Tongues is a supernatural utterance or unfamiliar language inspired by God. Tongues are an outward manifestation of an inward experience.

The Interpretation of Tongues is a God inspired supernatural revelation to interpret a message spoken in an unknown or an unfamiliar tongue or language.

Old Testament example:

Genesis 11:7-9- (cjb) *Come, let's (Elohim God- the Father, Son and Holy Spirit) go down and confuse their language, so that they won't understand each other's speech." 8 So from there ADONAI scattered them all over the earth, and they stopped building the city. 9 **For this reason it is called Bavel (confusion) - (our English word babbling originates from the root word Babel)** because there ADONAI confused the language of the whole earth, and from there ADONAI scattered them all over the earth.*

The French Academy found that there are 2,796 languages in the earth. This finding seems to support this scripture and also lay the ground work for the New Testament experience at Pentecost.

Acts 2: 4-11

*They were all filled with the Ruach HaKodesh and began to talk in different languages, as the Spirit enabled them to speak. 5 Now there were staying in Yerushalayim religious Jews from every nation under heaven. 6 **(The religious Jews that were in Jerusalem at the time. When they heard this sound, a crowd gathered; they were confused, much like the scene at Babel, because each one heard the believers speaking in his own language)**. 7 Totally amazed, they asked, "How is this possible? Aren't all these people who are speaking from the Galil?*

(Galilee) 8 How is it that we hear them speaking in our native languages? 9 We are Parthians, Medes, Elamites; residents of Mesopotamia, Y'hudah, Cappadocia, Pontus, Asia, 10 Phrygia, Pamphylia, Egypt, the parts of Libya near Cyrene; visitors from Rome; 11 Jews by birth and proselytes; Jews from Crete and from Arabia. . . ! How is it that we hear them speaking in our own languages about the great things God has done?"

This inspiration of language/tongues comes from God, the Father, the Son and Holy Spirit, as we saw in Genesis and now in Acts. How then can speaking in tongues be of the Devil? Those that had been baptized with the Holy Spirit began to speak with other tongues. Each person had the ability to speak in tongues but also had the ability to hear the interpretation of those tongues by those who spoke the language.

Jesus speaking to His disciples before His Ascension to Heaven in <u>Mark 16:15-17</u> says And these signs will accompany those who do trust/believe: in my name they will drive out demons, *speak with new tongues,*18 not be injured if they handle snakes or drink poison, and heal the sick by laying hands on them." 19 *So then, after he had spoken to them, the Lord Yeshua was taken up into heaven and sat at the right hand of God.* 20 And they went out and proclaimed everywhere, *the Lord working with them and confirming the message by the accompanying signs.* God the Holy Spirit demonstrates His gifts as the disciples went forth.

Question: What gifts are being revealed and identified?

Answer:

- Drive out demons- gift of discernment needed
- Tongues-obvious gift
- Handle snakes/drink poison- gift of faith needed
- Heal the sick- gift of healing and or working of miracles needed

Luke 11:11 is in response to someone who is seeking "bread" which signifies spiritual food or knowledge of the kingdom. That person who seeks diligently finds what he is looking for.

*Verse 11 then states: Is there any father here who, if his son asked him for a fish, would instead of a fish give him a snake? 12 Or if he asked for an egg would give him a scorpion? 13 So if you, even though you are bad, know how to give your children gifts that are good, how much more will the Father keep giving the **Ruach HaKodesh** from heaven to those who keep asking Him!"*

What am I saying: if you ask the Father for the Holy Spirit, the Holy Spirit and all of who He is, is given to those who ask. He comes with all of His gifts to those who want them!

What should we learn from 1 Corinthians 14 regarding speaking in tongues?

2 *For someone speaking in a tongue is not speaking to people but to God, because no one can understand, since he is uttering mysteries in the power of the Spirit.* **(It is the most intimate communion with the Father one can have. You are praying from your spirit to God's Spirit).** **4** *A person speaking in a tongue does edify himself,* **6** *Brothers, suppose I come to you now speaking in tongues. How can I be of benefit to you unless I bring you some revelation or knowledge or prophecy or teaching;* **some understanding of what I spoke?** **13** Therefore someone who speaks in a *tongue should pray for the power to interpret.* **14** *For if I pray in a tongue, my spirit does pray, but my mind is unproductive. (Bypassing natural intellect or reasoning)* **15** *so, what about it? I will pray with my spirit, but I will also pray with my mind; I will sing with my spirit, but I will also sing with my mind.* **18** *I thank God that I speak in tongues more than all of you,* **(Paul prayed a lot in tongues- I was thinking about all of his tests, trials and persecutions and yet he managed to finish his course and fulfill his purpose because he**

prayed in tongues a lot! For me this was a KEY to his success and ability to walk in power and authority in the earth).

19 but in a congregation meeting I would rather say five words with my mind in order to instruct others than ten thousand words in a tongue! **(So everyone can be encouraged/edified)**
20 Brothers, ***don't be children in your thinking.*** *In evil, be like infants; but in your thinking,* ***be grown-up.*** *21 In the Torah it is written, "By other tongues, by the lips of foreigners I will speak to this people. But even then they will not listen to me," says ADONAI. 22 Thus tongues are a sign not for believers but for unbelievers, while prophecy is not for unbelievers but for believers. 26 What is our conclusion, brothers? Whenever you come together, let everyone be ready with a psalm or a teaching or a revelation, or ready to use his gift of tongues or give an interpretation; but let everything be for edification. 27 If the gift of tongues is exercised, let it be by two or at most three, and each in turn; and let someone interpret. 28 And if there is no one present who can interpret, let the people who speak in tongues keep silent when the congregation meets - they can speak to themselves and to God.*
39 So, my brothers, eagerly seek to prophesy; ***and do not forbid speaking in tongues; 40 but let all things be done in a proper and orderly way.***

<u>**Jude: 20**</u> *But you, dear friends, build yourselves up in your most holy faith, and pray in union with the Ruach HaKodesh.* ***21 Thus keep yourselves in God's love,*** *as you wait for our Lord Yeshua the Messiah to give you the mercy that leads to eternal life.*

<u>**Romans 8:26-28**</u> *Similarly, the Spirit helps us in our weakness; for we don't know how to pray the way we should. But the Spirit himself pleads on our behalf with groanings* ***(mysteries spoken of in 1 Corinthians 14:2 – tongues)*** *too deep for words; 27 and the one who searches hearts knows exactly what the Spirit is thinking, because his pleadings for God's people accord with God's will. 28 Furthermore, we know that God causes everything to work together for the good of those who love God and are called in accordance with his purpose.*

Question: How do we have this assurance of the outcome of our prayers by praying in tongues?

<u>Answer: 1 John 5:14, 15</u>

14 This is the confidence we have in His Presence; if we ask anything that accords with his will, he hears us. **15** And if we know that he hears us - whatever we ask - then we know that we have what we have asked from him.

Section 3

IDENTIFYING YOUR MOTIVATIONAL GIFTS

Lesson 1

Ministerial Gifts vs Motivational Gifts

Ministerial Positions or Five-Fold Ministry

Not everyone functions in these offices or roles. These ministerial positions are usually demonstrated in a person's life and validated by God. <u>**Romans 11:29 (cjb)**</u> *says for God's free gifts and His calling are irrevocable; and are recognized by presbytery; presiding elders of a church body* as was the case with Timothy by Paul when he said in <u>**Philippians 2:20-22**</u> *But I trust in the Lord Jesus to send Timothy to you shortly, that I also may be encouraged when I know your state. **20** For I have no one like-minded, who will sincerely care for your state. **21 For all seek their own** (some have their own agenda), not the things which are of Christ Jesus. 22 **But you know his proven character, that as a son with his father he served with me in the gospel.**

<u>Ephesians 4:11 – Ministerial Roles</u>

- The role of the **Apostle** is to lay the foundation.
- The role of the **Prophet** is to be God's mouthpiece in the earth.
- The role of the **Evangelist** is to stir up people to win souls.
- The role of the **Pastor** is to shepherd and nurture the sheep.
- The role of the **Teacher** is to present Truth

Romans 12: 1-8 Motivational Spiritual Gifts

These gifts are for service or serving the body.

1 I exhort you, therefore, brothers, in view of God's mercies, to offer yourselves as a sacrifice, living and set apart for God. This will please him; it is the logical "Temple worship" for you.

2 In other words, do not let yourselves be conformed to the standards of **'olam hazeh Hebrew word meaning "this world in which you live.** *Instead, keep letting yourselves be transformed by the renewing of your minds; so that* **you will know what God wants** *and will agree that what he wants is good, satisfying and able to succeed.*

3 For I am telling every single one of you, through the grace that has been given to me, **not to have exaggerated ideas about your own importance.** *Instead, develop a sober estimate of yourself based on the standard which God has given to each of you, namely, trust.* **(In some translation this word is Faith)**

4 For just as there are many parts that compose one body, but the parts don't all have the same function; 5 so there are many of us, and in union with the Messiah we comprise one body, with each of us belonging to the others.
Simply stated:
1. There are many of us
2. We are unified in Christ
3. We make up one Body
4. Belong to each other

Question: So what does this mean and how does it apply to motivational spiritual gifts?

Answer: Ephesians 4:11 Jesus gave some people as emissaries or apostles, some as prophets, some as proclaimers or evangelists of the Good News, and some as shepherds or pastors and teachers. **These positions are ministerial.**

12 Their task is to equip God's people for the <u>work of service</u> that builds the body of the Messiah, **(We, believers, all have an assignment; we all have a place to function within the body)** *the work of service then* *becomes your motivational gifting's* **13** *until we all arrive at the unity implied by trusting and knowing the Son of God, at full manhood, at the standard of maturity set by the Messiah's perfection.* **In other words, until we are unified by our faith and knowledge of Jesus and the Word Christ is formed in us.**

Go back to **Romans 12:6** *But we have gifts that differ and which are meant to be used according to the grace that has been given to us.* **(The word Grace here implies God's divine influence on our heart and its reflection in our life).**

If we look at **Ephesians 4:7** (**cjb**) Each one of us, however, has been given grace **to be measured** by the Messiah's bounty. The New King James says: unto every one of us is given grace according to the **measure of the gift of Christ**.

What does this mean? It is our responsibility to develop and mature within the body with the aid of the motivational spiritual gifts. Let's substantiate this by looking at scripture.

Ephesians 4:16 (cjb) *Under His control (Jesus) the whole body is being fitted and held together* **by the support of every joint, with each part working to fulfill its function**; *this is how the body grows and builds itself up in love .*

Romans 12:6-8 (cjb)
So now; if your gift is **prophecy**, *use it to the extent of your trust; (prophecy according to the measure of your faith)* **7** *if it is* **serving**, *use it to serve; if you are a* **teacher,** *use your gift in teaching;* **8** *if you are a* **counselor or exhorter**, *use your gift to comfort and exhort; if you are someone who gives, do it simply and generously; if you are in a position of* **leadership or administrator,** *lead with diligence and zeal; if you are one who does acts of* **mercy**, *do them cheerfully.*

We all have natural talents and motivational spiritual gifting that are in our DNA which is our genetic coding. At the time of salvation they are more pronounced and are used by God to develop the believer to **see the needs** of others and **meet those needs**. The believer is then compelled to find his/her place in the church where the motivational spiritual gift can be recognized and exercised.

Look at <u>Ephesians 4:1-3</u>

*Therefore I, the prisoner united with the Lord, beg you to lead a life worthy of the **calling to which you have been called. (Some translations use the word vocation)** 2 Always be humble, gentle and patient, bearing with one another in love, 3 and making every effort to preserve the unity the Spirit gives through the binding power of shalom or peace. **(These are some of the fruit of the Spirit found in <u>Galatians 5:22</u>)** Our motivation to function in the body is predicated on the fruit developed in our life. 4 There is one body and one Spirit, just as when **you were called** (we were given a motivational spiritual gift) you were called to one hope. 5 And there is one Lord, one trust or faith, one immersion referring to the baptism in Christ, 6 and one God, the Father of all, who rules over all, works through all and is in all.*

Sidebar: This scripture also confirms for us as believers that there are not many paths to God there is only one way: One Body which is the Church; One Holy Spirit; One Hope which is the Christians calling; One Lord who is Jesus Christ; One Faith which is the message of the gospel; One God.

Regarding spiritual gifts, I want you to note that:

1. A believer might demonstrate more than one motivational spiritual gift but one will be more outstanding or dominant.

2. Motivational spiritual gifts are different from talents: A talent is the physical natural ability or aptitude of an individual. (For example: dancing, playing an instrument, writing etc.)

3. Motivational spiritual gifts help to direct us to our position in the body and help us to identify others in the body and where they function **(the bible says we are to know those who labor among us.)**

1 Thessalonians 5:11-15 therefore, *encourage each other, and build each other up;* **12** We ask you, brothers, *to respect those who are working hard among you, those who are guiding you in the Lord and confronting you in order to help you change.* **13** *Treat them with the highest regard* and love because of the work they are doing. *Live at peace among yourselves;* **14** *but we urge you, brothers, to confront those who are lazy, your aim being to help them change, to encourage the timid, to assist the weak, and to be patient with everyone.* **15** See that no one repays evil for evil; on the contrary, always try to do good to each other, indeed, to everyone.

4. There are seven motivational gifts which are Prophecy; Serving or Ministry of Helps; Teaching; Exhorting; Giving; Administration and Mercy.

Lesson 2

The Motivational Gift of Prophecy – Part 1

The 7 Motivational Spiritual Gifts found in Romans 12:1-8 are:

Prophecy
Serving (hospitality or ministry of helps)
Giving
Administration (to lead, rule, organizer)
Exhorting
Teaching
Mercy

Let's look at the Motivational Gifts one at a time:

Prophecy A person who functions with this gifting is a person who applies the Word of God to every situation for the purpose of exposing sin and restoring relationships. They have a strong sense of right and wrong and will speak out against the compromise of evil. They have a good sense about people and sometimes are labeled "intuitive "or "insightful".

The Goal:
1. To bring a person to accountability – important for them to have others to take ownership of situation; problem; crisis etc.
2. Expose motives
3. Bring heart conviction
4. Brings awareness of God's Presence
5. Repentance

Attributes or Traits of this type of Individual:

- There is a dependence on scriptural truth to validate authority-everything they speak into or about is backed up by the Word.

- They have experienced brokenness therefore prompting brokenness in others.

- They want to see outward evidence of an inward conviction.

- Always want to protect God's reputation.

- When speaking they are very direct and very persuasive.

- Eager to have others point out their own blind spots in order to help others. They are very transparent.

There is a difference between the Gift of Prophecy and the Motivational Gift of Prophecy. **The Gift of Prophecy is a supernatural utterance given by God that edifies, comforts and encourages and is available to everyone.** The Bible is the sure Word of Prophecy some of which has been fulfilled and some of which is yet to be fulfilled. The gift is usually on display in public meetings. **The Motivational Gift of Prophecy is applied to every situation, is individually focused to bring conviction and exposes sin in a person's life.**

We all have natural talents and motivational spiritual giftings that are in our DNA which is our genetic coding. The chromosomes are the blueprint or mapping of what we will look like; who we will be and what our bent or inclinations will be like. 50% of our chromosomes comes from our fathers and 50% come from our mothers. Our traits and personalities are spawn from our family history. As we grow and mature physically our natural talents are developed and cultivated. When we are born again spiritually, **the**

Holy Spirit empowers our motivational gifts and we become aware of their purpose. Our motivational gift then becomes a tool God uses to help us identify and meet the needs of others, as well as, help us to determine our placement in a particular body of believers where they will be recognized and utilized.

Let me say this, **our motive is the impetus for motivation and our motivation will shape our motivational gifts.** The root word motive comes from motivation and is defined as: something that causes a person to act a certain way, do a certain thing; the goal of a person's actions.

Let me give you an example:

It is well documented that Jesus existed before the World was formed- John 1: 1, 2 *In the beginning was the Word, and the Word was with God and the Word was God. 2* ***He was with God in the beginning.***

Genesis 1:26 Then God said. *"Let us make humankind in our image, in the likeness of ourselves; Genesis 11:7 – Come let us go down and confuse their language, so that they won't understand each other's speech."*

There is a record of Jesus's new birth experience – Luke 1: 35 The angel answered her, "The **Ruach HaKodesh** will come over you, the power of Ha`Elyon will cover you. Therefore the Holy child born to you will be called the Son of God.

Revelation: Jesus was in the beginning and was symbolically re-born into the world through the human channel.

John 3: 1-8 *Nicodemus is told he must be born again; he must have a new birth/born again experience.*

Remember I stated that after the new birth or born again experience the Holy Spirit empowers our motivational gifts, then we come to know their purpose.

<u>Acts 10:38</u> *God anointed Jesus of Nazareth with the Holy Spirit and power so that He went about **doing good (deeds), healing (compassion-Jesus was always moved with compassion or mercy)** all who were oppressed by the devil, for God was with Him.*

Question: What do we gain from this verse of scripture relative to motivational gifts?

Answer:

1. Holy Spirit – Spiritual Gifts

2. Power- Ministerial Position

3. Deeds – Motive

4. Compassion – Motivational Gift

Question: Is this revelation supported in scripture?

Answer:

Jesus functioned in union with the Holy Spirit and demonstrated the gifts of the Holy Spirit in His ministry – <u>**Luke 4:1**</u> *He was full of the Holy Spirit and **1 Corinthians 11,12** – One and the same Spirit is at work in all these things, distributing to each person as he chooses. For just as the body is one but has many parts; and all the parts of the body, though many, constitute one body; so it is with the Messiah.*

<u>**Jesus's Ministerial Positions:**</u>

Apostle – laying the foundation – <u>**Matthew 16:18**</u> (the church is built upon the "Rock" which is the revelation of who Jesus is)

Prophet – mouth piece of God – <u>**Matthew 13:57**</u>; (prophet is not without honor except in his own country) <u>**John 14:10**</u> (only spoke what the Father told Him to speak)

Evangelist – harvester of souls – <u>**Luke 10: 1, 2;**</u> (He sent out the 70 to cities where He too was going to gather the harvest)

Pastor- shepherd of the sheepfold – **John 10: 11, 14**; (He knows His sheep)

Teacher- presenter of truth – **John 14:16** (He is the Way, the Truth and Life)

Question: Did He have a Motive?

Answer:

In the beginning God said in **Genesis 3:15**, that He would put enmity (hostility, hatred, antagonism, ill will) between Satan and his seed and the woman and her seed. In **Ephesians 2:15-18** – Jesus used his flesh to abolish the law thereby creating in Himself one new man from Himself (2ⁿᵈ Adam) to reconcile both Himself and Adam/mankind to God in one body through the cross thereby putting to death the enmity, giving us access by one Spirit to the Father. His motive was clearly reconciliation and restoration!

Personal Study: Jesus' Motivational Gifts – Read and Reflect

Compassion/ Mercy – Matthew 9:36; Matthew 18:27; Mark 1:41

Teaching – Matthew 8:19; Matthew 12:38; Matthew 19:16

Serving – Matthew 20:28 or Mark 10:45

Administration – Luke 22:8

Exhorter – John 14:25-31; John 15:11-17

Giving – John 3:16

Prophecy – Matthew 15:1-14, Matthew 12;17-21, Matthew 16: 1-4

Knowing that these gifts are for service or serving the body according to **Romans 12: 1-8** and according to **Ephesians 4:16** we can understand how under the control of Jesus the whole body can and will be fitted and held together **by the support of every joint, with each part working to fulfill its function.**

- A believer might demonstrate more than one motivational spiritual gift but one will be more outstanding or dominant.
- Motivational spiritual gifts are different from talents. A talent is the physical natural ability or aptitude of an individual. (For example: dancing, playing an instrument, writing etc.)

Again, the **Motivational Gift of Prophecy** operating in a person who functions with this gifting is a person who applies the Word of God to every situation for the purpose of exposing sin and restoring relationships. This gift is also referred to as the **"eye of the body"**.

Question: Can you name one of Jesus' followers who operated in this capacity and list the scripture or scriptures that support your answer?

Personal Study: Read and **List** the attributes or traits of this motivational gift.

John the Baptist – Luke 3:3-20; Matthew 3:1-12

Peter – Acts 2:14-39

Lesson 3

The Motivational Gift of Prophecy - Part 2

REVIEW ~ RUMINATE~ REFLECT

In the previous lesson we discussed the difference between the **Gift of_Prophecy and the Motivational Gift of Prophecy**. The **Gift of Prophecy** is a supernatural utterance given by God that edifies, comforts and encourages and is available to everyone. The **Motivational Gift of Prophecy** is individually focused to bring conviction and expose sin in a person's life. This gift is also referred to as the **"eye of the body"**.

A person's motive will be the impetus for motivation and motivation will shape ones motivational gift. Therefore motivation is something that causes a person to act in a certain way and/or do a certain thing. It can be the person's primary goal in life and be exhibited in their consistent actions or behavior.

We know that these gifts are for serving the body according to **Romans 12: 1-8;** *but under the control of Jesus, the whole body will be fitted and held together by the support of every joint, with each part working to fulfill its function according_to **Ephesians 4:16***

Is it a motivational spiritual gift or talent?

Motivational spiritual gifts are different from talents. Talents are the physical natural ability or aptitude of an individual whereas motivational spiritual gifts help direct us to our position in the body and help us to identify others in the body and where they function. It is not uncommon for us to demonstrate more than one spiritual gift.

Let me say this, *some* reasons why we don't know or recognize our motivational gifts could be because:

1. There is known sin in our lives.

2. We might be trying to imitate someone else's gift.

3. We are not involved in a local body; not connected to other believers.

4. Have not learned how to identify your giftedness or lack of teaching.

The Motivational Gift of Prophecy – The eye of the Body

A person who demonstrates the motivational gift of Prophecy is a person who always applies the Word of God to every situation for the purpose of exposing sin and restoring relationships. Because they have a strong sense of right and wrong they will always speak out against evil refusing to compromise truth. You will find that these individuals are very intuitive and or perceptive. God places a greater responsibility on them to have clear and sound vision. That is one reason this gift is referred to as the "eyes of the body". **They need to be able to see and discern God's truths and share what they see without the truth being contaminated, defiled or polluted.** Thus, they cannot afford to have impurity in their lives rendering cloudy and impaired vision. Seeing through a lens that is impaired or cloudy will make them prone to error, which will lead others to go astray. Dan and Katie Fortune point out the error of Jim Jones as an example of this.

Additional Attributes or Traits of this type of Individual:

- There is a dependence on scriptural truth to validate authority-everything they speak into or about is backed up by the Word. The Word is in their opinion the only authority.

- They operate solely on Bible principles which enable them to extrapolate truths that are applicable to daily and righteous living.

- They have experienced brokenness therefore prompting brokenness in others.

- They believe in and look for outward evidence of one's inward conviction.

- Very protective of God's reputation.

- When speaking they are very direct, blunt, do not mince words and are very persuasive. Their persuasiveness comes from a strong sense of conviction. Their stance is either black or white with no gray areas or middle ground.

- Not afraid to be transparent, therefore illicit having their blind spots identified in order to help others.

- Desire to be obedient at all cost.

Our example of this gift is illustrated in the person of John the Baptist <u>Luke 3:3-20 (cjb)</u>

3 *He went all through the Yarden (Jordan) region proclaiming an immersion* ***(water baptism)*** *involving turning to God from sin in order to be forgiven.* 4 *It was just as had been written in the book of the sayings of the prophet Yesha`yahu,* ***(Isaiah)*** *"The voice of someone crying out: `In the desert prepare the way for ADONAI!* ***(Lord of Host)*** *Make straight paths for him!* 5 *Every valley must be filled in, every mountain and hill leveled off; the winding roads must be straightened and the rough ways made smooth.* 6 *Then all humanity will see God's deliverance.'"*

VERSES 4-6 John knew he was the voice of God so he was very dependent upon scriptural truth to validate his authority.

7 *Therefore, Yochanan* ***(John)*** *said to the crowds who came out to be immersed by him, "You snakes! Who warned you to escape the coming punishment?* 8 *If you have really turned from your sins, produce fruit that will prove it! And don't start saying to yourselves, `Avraham* ***(Abraham)*** *is*

*our father'! For I tell you that God can raise up for Avraham (**Abraham**) sons from these stones!*

VERSES 7-8 **John was very blunt and direct in his confrontation. He discerned their motives and wanted outward evidence of their inward conviction.**

9 *Already the axe is at the root of the trees, ready to strike; every tree that doesn't produce good fruit will be chopped down and thrown in the fire!"* **10** *The crowds asked Yochanan, "So then, what we should do?"* **11** *He answered, "Whoever has two coats should share with somebody who has none, and whoever has food should do the same."* **12** *Tax-collectors also came to be immersed; and they asked him, "Rabbi, what should we do?"* **13** *"Collect no more than the government assesses," he told them.* **14** *Some soldiers asked him, "What about us? What should we do?" To them he said, "Don't intimidate anyone, don't accuse people falsely, and be satisfied with your pay."*

VERSES 10-14 **John is looking for repentance from the people.**

15 *The people were in a state of great expectancy, and everyone was wondering whether perhaps Yochanan himself might be the Messiah;* **16** *so Yochanan answered them all, "I am immersing you in water, but he who is coming is more powerful than I. I'm not worthy to untie his sandals! He will immerse you in the **Ruach HaKodesh** and in fire.* **17** *He has with him his winnowing fork to clear out his threshing floor and gather his wheat into his barn, but he will burn up the straw with unquenchable fire!"*

VERSES 16, 17 **John is very much aware of his own unworthiness making him open for correction.**

18 *And with many other warnings besides these he announced the Good News to the people.* **19** *But Yochanan also denounced Herod the regional governor for taking as his own wife Herodias, the wife of his brother, and for* *all the other wicked things Herod had done; 20 whereupon Herod added this to the rest: he locked up Yochanan in prison.*

VERSES 18-20 John was not afraid to confront the sins of Herod, therefore taking a stand against evil and emphasizing what's right and what is wrong. John was thrown into prison and eventually beheaded for his strong position.

Matthew 14: 3-8 (cjb)   *For Herod had arrested Yochanan, put him in chains and thrown him in prison because of Herodias, the wife of his brother Philip; 4 since Yochanan had told Herod, "It violates the Torah for you to have her as your wife." 5 Herod had wanted to put Yochanan to death; but he was afraid of the people, in whose eyes he was a prophet. 6 However, at Herod's birthday celebration, Herodias' daughter danced before the company and pleased Herod 7 so much that he promised with an oath to give her whatever she asked. 8 Prompted by her mother, she said, "Give me here on a platter the head of Yochanan the Immerser.* **(John the Baptizer).**

Misunderstandings of the Motivational Gift of Prophecy

- Their blunt and sometimes harsh assessment of situations and or circumstances can seem insensitive and judgmental.
- Their desire to see results may appear to be gimmicky or dramatic.
- Their boldness and stringent standards often hinder personal relationships, others seem to be intimidated by their very presence.
- Their strong desire to communicate truths may be interpreted as rejecting the opinions of others.
- They are dogmatic about one's personal spiritual growth, failing to allow individuals to take small steps progressively.

Individuals who demonstrate the **Motivational Gift of Prophecy** are usually convinced that their view is right and they usually are...BUT

....they need to learn to value other motivational gifts that might render another point of view based upon perception or facets of truths in a given situation or circumstance.

Remember I Corinthians 12:12-26, we are unified yet diverse, we are one body and we are to demonstrate care for one another so that there will be no schisms in the body. As a part of the body of Christ you might be moved to minister to others regardless of your gifting anytime or anyplace. Don't ever let your knowledge of your particular motivational gift keep you from ministering in other areas. Always be guided by the Holy Spirit to do so.

Lesson 4

The Motivational Gifts of Serving

There are 7 Motivational Spiritual Gifts found in Romans 12: 1-8

Prophecy

Serving (hospitality or ministry of helps)

Giving

Administration (to lead; rule; organize)

Exhorting

Teaching

Mercy (compassion)

In this lesson we are going to look at the **Motivational Gift of Serving** or as some call **"the ministry of helps "**.

<u>**The Motivational Gift of Serving - The hand of the body**</u>

If we believe that a person's motive will be the impetus for motivation and motivation will shape ones motivational gift then <u>what motivates</u> an individual who functions in the motivational gift of serving or the ministry of helps? A person with the gift of serving takes great pleasure in helping or assisting others; they do not mind carrying out instructions and can be useful in a wide variety of tasks.

<u>**Attributes or Traits of this type of Individual**</u>

- They are quick to identify and meet the needs of others.
- They express or demonstrate their love for others by their works or deeds.
- They enjoy working with their hands.
- They enjoy entertaining or hosting events.

- They are perfectionists.
- They will not leave a project or task until it is completed.
- They are a great support to leadership.
- They always go above and beyond the call of duty.
- They want to be appreciated for their efforts.
- They enjoy short term assignments over long term assignments.
- They over-commit themselves- it's hard for them to say no.

Matthew 20:26-28 / Mark 10:45 says (**Jesus speaking**) *whoever among you wants to be a leader must become your servant, 27 and whoever wants to be first must be your slave! 28 For the Son of Man did not come to be served, but **to serve** and **to give** his life as a ransom for many."*

John 21:3-12 (Jesus is serving his disciples)

Shim`on Kefa (**Simon Peter**) *said, "I'm going fishing."* They said to him, *"We're coming with you."* They went and got into the boat, but that night they didn't catch anything. 4 **just as day was breaking, Yeshua stood on shore, but the talmidim (disciples) didn't know it was he. 5 He said to them, "You don't have any fish, do you?" "No," they answered him. 6 He said to them, "Throw in your net to starboard and you will catch some." So they threw in their net, and there were so many fish in it that they couldn't haul it aboard. 9 When they stepped ashore, they saw a fire of burning coals with a fish on it, and some bread._10 Yeshua said to them, "Bring some of the fish you have just caught."** 11 *Shim`on Kefa* (**Simon Peter**) *went up and dragged the net ashore. It was full of fish, 153 of them; but even with so many, the net wasn't torn. 12 Yeshua said to them, "**Come and have breakfast."***

Old Testament Example:

Shunammite Woman- 2 Kings 4:8-13

8 One day Elisha visited Shunem, and a well-to-do woman living there pressed him to stay and eat a meal. **(She was hospitable)** After this, whenever he came through, he stopped there for a meal. **(She must have enjoyed entertaining Elisha, because every time he was in her city she had a meal ready for him).**9 She said to her husband, "I can see that this is a holy man of God who keeps stopping at our place. **(She was able to see the need) 10** Please, let's build him a little room on the roof. We'll put a bed and a table in it for him, and a stool and a candlestick. **(She had a detailed plan that was perfect)** Then, whenever he comes to visit us, he can stay there." **11** One day Elisha came to visit there, and he went into the upper room to lie down. **12** He said to Geichazi his servant, "Call this Shunamite." He called her; and when she arrived, **13** he said to him, "Tell her this: **'You have shown us so much hospitality! What can I do to show my appreciation? She is appreciated and rewarded.**

Elisha himself, also operated in *serving* or the **ministry of helps** to Elijah **1 Kings 19:19-21**

New Testament Examples:

Phoebe, Priscilla and Aquila, Urbanus, **Tryphaena and Tryphosa** **Romans 16:1-5, 9, 12** *I am introducing to you our sister Phoebe, shammash (servant) of the congregation at Cenchrea, 2 so that you may welcome her in the Lord, as God's people should, and give her whatever assistance she may need from you;* **for she has been a big help to many people; including myself.** *3 Give my greetings to* **Priscilla and Aquila, my fellow workers for the Messiah Yeshua.** *4 They risked their necks to save my life; not only I thank them, but also all the Messianic communities* *among the Gentiles.* **5** *And give my greetings to the congregation that meets in their house.* **9** *Greetings to Urbanus, our fellow worker for the Messiah,* and to my dear friend Stachys. **12** *Greet Tryphaena and Tryphosa, women who are working hard for the Lord. Greet my dear friend Persis, another woman who has done a lot of hard work for the Lord.*

Timothy and Epaphroditus **Philippians 2: 19-30**

Martha **Luke 10: 38-42 (nlt)**

38 Jesus and the disciples continued on their way to Jerusalem, they came to a certain village where a woman named *Martha welcomed him into her home. Martha demonstrated her hospitality* **39** Her sister, Mary, sat at the Lord's feet, listening to what he taught. **40** But Martha was distracted by the big dinner she was preparing. She came to Jesus and said, "Lord, doesn't it seem unfair to you that my sister just sits here while I do all the work? Tell her to come and help me."

VERSE 40 She recognized the need to feed Jesus and his disciples but she has over committed to the point she wanted help from her sister Mary.

41 But the Lord said to her, "My dear Martha, you are worried and upset over all these details!

VERSE 41 The perfectionist comes out and she may feel unappreciated for all of her hard work without her sister's help.

42 There is only one thing worth being concerned about. Mary has discovered it, and it will not be taken away from her."

VERSE 42 Martha let the details get in the way of what was really important; she was focusing on the short term goal of feeding her guest and neglected the long term goal of realizing Jesus was headed to the cross and time spent with Him was more important than a physical/natural meal.

Misunderstandings of the Motivational Gift of Serving

- Can be very critical of others when others do not help to meet needs.
- They try to help when their help is not wanted or needed, so help comes off as being pushy.
- They do all the work themselves instead of delegating some of the tasks.
- Easily offended when they are not appreciated.
- Their families get overlooked or neglected because they are too busy meeting needs of others.
- Hard to accept serving from others.
- Serves to get affection and or attention from others.

I believe that there should be a little bit of this gift working in all of us, without it being a dominant gifting.

Remember: For the Son of Man did not come to be served, but to serve and to give and we should find opportunities to do the same.

Personal Study Question: Our next lesson we will cover the Motivational Gift of Giving, so can you name (1) Old Testament Giver with specific scriptures that reference his or her giving?

Lesson 5

The Motivational Gift of Giving

There are 7 Motivational Spiritual Gifts found in Romans 12: 1-8

Prophecy

Serving (hospitality or ministry of helps)

Giving

Administration (to lead; rule; organize)

Exhorting

Teaching

Mercy (compassion)

So far in this study we have covered the **Motivational Gift of Prophecy** which is considered the **"eye of the body"** and the **Motivational Gift of Serving** which is considered to be the **"hand of the body"**. In this lesson, we are going to look at the **Motivational Gift of Giving** which is considered to be the **"arm of the body"**.

The Motivational Gift of Giving - The arm of the Body

I thought that this was an interesting statement made by Don and Katie Fortune. They say **"of all the seven motivational gifts; this one is the least likely to be identified by the one who has the gift."** They are not usually one to broadcast their giving to others which is attributed to the giver's personality. These individuals enjoy meeting needs behind the scene without any fanfare. Their giving is usually done anonymously and are grateful when they find meeting the need was an answer to someone's prayer.

Attributes or Traits of this type of Individual

- Givers are tithers **(this is just foundational in their mindset)** and usually give beyond 10% of their income.
- They give generously of their money, possessions and their time.
- They take no credit nor seek to be applauded for their giving.
- They go to great lengths to keep their giving a secret.
- They usually partner with ministries that are effectively impacting the lives of people who are promoting the message of the kingdom.
- They tend to function in the role of intercessor because of the burden they have for the souls of people.
- They have the ability to make wise purchases and investments. They are not consumer driven, they are investment driven.
- They possess good stewardship skills, demonstrating wisdom, caution and prudence.
- Their giving motivates others to do the same.
- They wait for the Holy Spirit's leading to give, therefore not pressured into giving by appeals.
- Their gift giving is of high quality but within their capacity.
- They are natural and successful business leaders.

Matthew 20: 28 Jesus said "For the Son of Man did not come to be served, but _to serve_ and _to give_ his life as a ransom for many." The characteristics might look the same for both but the inward viewpoint is different. The individual with the **Motivational Gift of Serving sees hospitality as a chance to serve. On the other hand, the giver also loves to practice hospitality but sees it as an opportunity to give.**

Personal Study Reading: Old Testament Example of Givers:

- **Solomon   1 Kings 3: 12, 13, 16-28; 1 Kings 4:29-34, 1 Kings Chapters 8, 9, 10**

Abraham has a compelling history of giving, so let's take a look at the ways he gave.

Genesis 13: 2-16 (nkjv) 2 Abram was very rich in livestock, in silver, and in gold.

VERSE 2 Validation of Abraham's wealth and success.

3 And he went on his journey from the South as far as Bethel, to the place where his tent had been at the beginning, between Bethel and Ai, 4 to the place of the altar which he had made there at first. And there Abram called on the name of the Lord. 5 Lot also, who went with Abram, had flocks and herds and tents. 6 Now the land was not able to support them that they might dwell together, for their possessions were so great that they could not dwell together.

VERSES 4-6: Because Abraham was blessed Lot (his nephew) shared in the blessings of Abraham by association.

7 And there was strife between the herdsmen of Abram's livestock and the herdsmen of Lot's livestock. The Canaanites and the Perizzites then dwelt in the land. 8 So Abram said to Lot, "Please let there be no strife between you and me, and between my herdsmen and your herdsmen; for we are brethren. 9 Is not the whole land before you? Please separate from me. If you take the left, then I will go to the right; or, if you go to the right, then I will go to the left."

VERSES 7-9: Abraham uses wisdom in separating the two camps. He gives Lot the best of the land. He was very generous toward Lot and Lot's family.

VERSES 14-16 After Abraham separates himself from Lot, God multiplies Abraham's wealth by giving him land in the North, South, East and West.

<u>Genesis 14: 14-23 (cjb)</u> **14** *When Avram heard that his nephew had been taken captive, he led out his trained men, who had been born in his house, 318 of them, and went in pursuit as far as Dan.* **15** *During the night he and his servants divided his forces against them, then attacked and pursued them all the way to Hovah, north of Dammesek.* **16** *He recovered all the goods and brought back his nephew Lot with his goods, together with the women and the other people.*

VERSES 14-16 Abraham goes to help Lot escape from his captors. He is successful in his endeavor.

17 *After his return from slaughtering K'dorla'omer and the kings with him, the king of S'dom (Sodom) went out to meet him in the Shaveh Valley, also known as the King's Valley.* **18** ***Malki-Tzedek (Melchizedek)*** *king of **Shalem (Salem)** brought out bread and wine. He was **Cohen (priest)** of **El 'Elyon (God Most High)**,* **19** *so he blessed him with these words: "Blessed be Avram by El 'Elyon, **(God Most High)** maker of heaven of earth.* **20** *and blessed be El 'Elyon, who handed your enemies over to you." Avram gave him a tenth of everything.*

VERSES 18-20: Institution of the first tithe recorded in the Bible, but also indicative of Abraham honoring God with his possessions. Receives the "Priestly Blessing".

21 *The king of S'dom (Sodom) said to Avram, "Give me the people, and keep the goods for yourself."* **22** *But Avram answered the king of S'dom (Sodom), "I have raised my hand in an oath to **ADONAI, El 'Elyon, (Sovereign, God Most High)** maker of heaven and earth,* **23** *that I will not take so much as a thread or a sandal thong of anything that is yours; so that you won't be able to say, 'I made Avram rich.'* **24** *I will take only what my* *troops have eaten and the share of the spoil belonging to the men who came with me - 'Aner, Eshkol and Mamre; let them have their share."*

VERSES 21-24 Abraham's wisdom not to compromise the things of the kingdom for the things of the world.

NOTE: <u>Genesis 18: 16-33 Abraham makes intercession for Sodom and Gomorrah.</u> Abraham pleads with God by asking if there were 50, 45, 40 30, 20, 10 righteous men would he spare Sodom and Gomorrah. He had a burden for the righteous people who lived among the sin and depravity of the Sodomites. He wanted God to spare the righteous and Lot his cousin was among them.

Genesis 22: 1-17 Abraham gives his best gift

*He said, "Take your son, your only son, whom you love, **Yitz'chak; (Isaac)** and go to the land of **Moriyah.(Moriah)** There you are to offer him as a burnt offering on a mountain that I will point out to you." 3 Avraham got up early in the morning, saddled his donkey, and took two of his young men with him, together with **Yitz'chak (Isaac)** his son. He cut the wood for the burnt offering, departed and went toward the place God had told him about. 4 On the third day, Avraham raised his eyes and saw the place in the distance.*
5 Avraham said to his young men, "Stay here with the donkey. I and the boy will go there, worship and return to you."

VERSE 5 Abraham honors God and withholds nothing from God. He has faith in God as his source and provision.

*6 Avraham took the wood for the burnt offering and laid it on **Yitz'chak (Isaac)** his son. Then he took in his hand the fire and the knife, and they both went on together. 7 **Yitz'chak (Isaac)** spoke to Avraham his father: "My father?" He answered, "Here I am, my son." He said, "I see the fire and the wood, but where is the lamb for a burnt offering?" 8 Avraham replied, "**God will provide himself the lamb for a burnt offering**, my son"; and they* *both went on together. (Abraham still has confidence in God's provision)* **9** *They came to the place God had told him about; and Avraham built the altar there, set the wood in order, bound Yitz'chak* **(Isaac)** *his son and laid him on the altar, on the wood.* **10** *Then Avraham put out his hand and took the knife to kill his son.* **11** *But the angel of ADONAI called to him out of heaven: "Avraham? Avraham!* "He answered, "Here I am." **12** *He said, "Don't lay your hand on the boy! Don't do anything to him! For now I know that you are a man who fears God, because you have not withheld your son, your only son, from me."* **13** *Avraham raised his eyes and looked, and there behind him was a ram caught in the bushes by its horns. Avraham went and took the ram and offered it up as a burnt offering in place of his son.* **14** *Avraham called the place ADONAI Yir'eh (Sovereign God Provider) ADONAI (Sovereign God will see to it, ADONAI (Sovereign God provides) as it is said to this day, "On the mountain ADONAI Sovereign God is seen."*

The Jewish people always wanted a sign from God of His Presence, even today. Jews need a sign for them to believe. They fully understand what it means to be in Covenant.

15 *The angel of ADONAI called to Avraham a second time out of heaven.* **16** *He said, "I have sworn by myself says ADONAI, that because you have done this,* **because you haven't withheld your son, your only son,** **17** *I will most certainly bless you; and I will most certainly increase your descendants to as many as there are stars in the sky or grains of sand on the seashore. Your descendants will possess the cities of their enemies.*

<u>Personal Study Reading: New Testament Examples:</u>

- **Cornelius -** <u>Acts 10: 1-31</u>

- **Mary Magdalene, Joanna, Susanna, Mary, (James' mom)** <u>Luke 8: 3,</u> <u>Luke 24:10</u>

- **Zacchaeus -** <u>Luke 19: 1-9</u>

174

Misunderstandings of the Motivational Gift of Serving

- Wants to take control of how contributions should be distributed, designated or utilized.
- Can and will sometimes put pressure on others to give to projects that are important to the individual because they see or believe in the value in the investment.
- May frustrate or anger family because of their spontaneous giving.
- Will offer financial gifts as a way of escaping the project or responsibility of other tasks.

Personal Study Question: **In our next lesson we will cover the Motivational Gift of Administration. Can you identify two people in the Old Testament that have the traits of an Administrator with scripture references?**

Joanne M. Green

176

Lesson 6

The Motivational Gift of Administration

The 7 Motivational Spiritual Gifts are found in Romans 12: 1-8

Prophecy

Serving (hospitality or ministry of helps)

Giving

Administration (to lead; rule; organize)

Exhortation

Teaching

Mercy (compassion)

In previous lessons we have discovered that the **Motivational Gift of Prophecy** is referred to as the **"eye of the body"**; the **Motivational Gift of Serving** is referred to as the **"hand of the body"** and the **Motivational Gift of Giving** is referred to as the **"arm of the body"**. In this lesson we will focus on *the Motivational Gift of Administration* which is referred to as the **"shoulder of the body "**. **Administrators** are almost always **"natural born leaders"**. They are duly gifted and talented in their ability to lead and organize others to coalesce around a single project, a ministry or an organization.

The Motivational Gift of Administration - The shoulder of the Body

Revelation 11:15 (cjb) states, The seventh angel sounded his shofar; and there were loud voices in heaven, saying, "The kingdom of the world has become the Kingdom of our Lord and his Messiah, and **He will rule forever and ever!"**

Isaiah 9:6 **(cjb)** *For a child is born to us, a son is given to us;* **dominion will rest on his shoulders,** *and he will be given the name Pele-Yo'etz El Gibbor Avi-'Ad Sar-Shalom meaning* **(Wonder of a Counselor, Mighty God, Father of Eternity, Prince of Peace), 7 in order to extend the dominion and perpetuate the peace of the throne and kingdom of David, to secure it and sustain it through justice and righteousness henceforth and forever.** *The zeal of ADONAI-Tzva'ot (Sovereign Lord of Host) will accomplish this.* **We saw this accomplished throughout Jesus's ministry on the earth.**

The prophet Isaiah prophetically states in **Isaiah 9:6** that Jesus, the Son of man born of a woman would be responsible to rule and reign in the earth. He would bear the burden of bringing men out of darkness into the marvelous light of the gospel. **He would administrate an earthly kingdom after the pattern of the heavenly kingdom** which supports or agree with the statement made in **Revelations 11:15.** So an individual who is motivated to rule, to lead or to govern shoulders the responsibility of getting things done that benefit the expansion of the kingdom. These natural born leaders are yoked to Jesus like an oxen is yoked to its plow.

Attributes or Traits of this type of Individual

- They are natural born leaders.
- They will not assume responsibility unless it has been delegated to them by someone in authority.
- They will assume a leadership role **only** if there is no apparent leader.
- They respect authority and therefore are given authority.
- They are highly motivated to organize a task that they are responsible for.
- They have great zeal and enthusiasm for their projects.
- They delegate and supervise people skillfully.
- They enjoy the long term goals versus the short term goals.

- They thrive on challenging projects or missions.
- These individuals are visionaries and know how to cast the vision for buy in.
- They are effective communicators.
- They handle criticism well for the sake of the goal being completed.
- They want to see projects be accomplished as quickly as possible.
- They easily manage resources and people effectively in order to complete a task or project.

Personal Study : Old Testament Example of Administrators:

- **Deborah – <u>Judges 4-5</u>**
- **David – <u>1 Samuel chapters 16-30</u>; the book of 2 Samuel**
- **Joseph – <u>Genesis 30-40</u>**
- **Nehemiah – <u>Nehemiah 1-7</u>**

I want to quickly summarize some of Nehemiah's characteristics as an Administrator. The Bible says Nehemiah had great concern for the welfare of the people of Jerusalem and because his **"burden"** was for the plight of the people living in great distress and reproach, he was prompted to take **bold and quick action** to rebuild what was broken and torn down. Nehemiah completed the task of rebuilding the wall of Jerusalem in only 52 days <u>**Nehemiah 6: 15**</u>, **in spite of the opposition and criticism** from within and without the city. Sanballat was mocking and criticizing his efforts <u>**Nehemiah 4:1**</u>. **Nehemiah was given authority and resources** to accomplish this monumental task from King Artaxerxes. <u>**Nehemiah chapter 2**</u> He was up to the challenge and took great pains to identify his army of volunteers to get the job done. **"For the people had a mind to work"** <u>**Nehemiah 4:6**</u>. After the wall was built Nehemiah spent his entire life reviving and reforming the people. He became a great Governor and leader.

Now let's turn our attention to Joseph

<u>Genesis chapters 37- 41 (cjb) 5</u> *Yosef had a dream which he told his* **brothers**, *and that made them hate him all the more.* 6 *He said to them, "Listen while I tell you about this dream of mine.* 7 *We were tying up bundles of wheat in the field when suddenly my bundle got up by itself and stood upright; then your bundles came, gathered around mine and prostrated themselves before it."* **8 His brothers retorted, "Yes, you will certainly be our king. You'll do a great job of bossing us around!"** *And they hated him still more for his dreams and for what he said.* 9 *He had another dream which he told his brothers: "***Here, I had another dream***, and there were the sun, the moon and eleven stars prostrating themselves before me."* **10 He told his father too, as well as his brothers, but his father rebuked him:** *"What is this dream you have had? Do you really expect me, your mother and your brothers to come and prostrate ourselves before you on the ground?"*

<u>VERSE 8-10</u> **Joseph's dream gives him vision; he cast his vision before his family for them to buy into his assignment. His zeal invites criticism among his brothers and parents. He is not deterred from what he envisioned. He will emerge as a leader.**

<u>Genesis 39:1-6</u> *Yosef was brought down to Egypt, and Potifar, an officer of Pharaoh's and captain of the guard, an Egyptian, bought him from the Yishma'elim who had brought him there.* 2 *ADONAI was with Yosef, and he* **became wealthy** *while he was in the household of his master the Egyptian.* **3 His master saw how ADONAI was with him, that ADONAI prospered everything he did. 4 Yosef pleased him as he served him, and his master appointed him manager of his household; he entrusted all his possessions to Yosef.** 5 *From the time he appointed him manager of his household and all his possessions, ADONAI blessed the Egyptian's household for Yosef's sake; ADONAI's blessing was on all he owned, whether in the house or in the field.* 6 *So he left all his possessions in*

Yosef's care; and because he had him, he paid no attention to his affairs, except for the food he ate.

Verses 3-6 Joseph's leadership abilities are on display; his organizational skills were evident based upon his success; he is operating under delegated authority.

<u>Genesis 41:25-43</u> *Yosef said to Pharaoh, "The dreams of Pharaoh are* **the same: God has told Pharaoh what he is about to do.** *26 The seven good cows are seven years, and the seven good ears of grain are seven years - the dreams are the same. 27 Likewise the seven lean and miserable-looking cows that came up after them are seven years, and also the seven empty ears blasted by the east wind - there will be seven years of famine. 28 This is what I told Pharaoh: God has shown Pharaoh what he is about to do.* **29 Here it is: there will be seven years of abundance throughout the whole land of Egypt;** *30 but afterwards, there will come seven years of famine; and Egypt will forget all the abundance. The famine will consume the land, 31 and the abundance will not be known in the land because of the famine that will follow, because it will be truly terrible. 32 Why was the dream doubled for Pharaoh? Because the matter has been fixed by God, and God will shortly cause it to happen.* **33 "Therefore, Pharaoh should look for a man both discreet and wise to put in charge of the land of Egypt. 34 Pharaoh should do this,** *and he should appoint supervisors over the land to* **receive a twenty percent tax on the produce of the land of Egypt during the seven years of abundance. 35 They should gather all the food produced during these good years coming up and set aside grain under the supervision of Pharaoh to be used for food in the cities, and they should store it. 36 This will be the land's food supply for the seven years of famine that will come over the land of Egypt, so that the land will not perish as a result of the famine."**

Verses: 33-36 Joseph is motivated to organize Pharoah's food supply. His plan is a long range plan lasting 14 years which is a challenge. Remember, administrators love a challenge! This project is monumental but Joseph sees the goal accomplished before it is even started. He had the vision.

37 The proposal seemed good both to Pharaoh and to all his officials. 38 Pharaoh said to his officials, "Can we find anyone else like him? The Spirit of God lives in him!" **39 So Pharaoh said to Yosef, "Since God has shown you all this - there is no one as discerning and wise as you - 40 you will be in charge of my household; all my people will be ruled by what you say. Only when I rule from my throne will I be greater than you." 41 Pharaoh said to Yosef, "Here, I place you in charge of the whole land of Egypt."** *42 Pharaoh took his signet ring off his hand and put it on Yosef's hand, had him clothed in fine linen with a gold chain around his neck 43 and had him ride in his second best chariot; and they cried before him, "Bow down!" Thus he placed him in charge of the whole land of Egypt.*

<u>Verses: 39- 43</u> Joseph is given a new level of power and authority by being elevated to a position that puts him 2nd in command. His promotion was the result of his motivational gift of administration or organizational skills. When you read Joseph's story in its entirety you note that his character and his leadership abilities are depicted throughout his tenure as a slave and servant.

<u>Personal Study Reading: New Testament Examples:</u>

- **Jairus- <u>Mark 5:22-24, 35-43; Luke 8:40-42; 49-56</u>**

- **The Centurion- <u>Matthew 8: 5-13; Luke 7: 2-10</u>**

- **Cornelius- <u>Acts 10:1-8; 21-33</u>**

<u>Misunderstandings of the Motivational Gift of Administration</u>

- Viewing people as resources or commodities may appear insensitive to the needs of the people. This can happen because they are so goal oriented or focused.
- Delegating tasks might be construed as "laziness".

- They tend to be viewed as "callous individuals. Because they have been constantly criticized they have "a thick skin" mentality.
- Will become upset or frustrated when people don't have the same vision.
- They are self-driven to their own detriment and the detriment of family.
- Because they love the thrill of their projects, they tend to neglect the mundane tasks of home life.

Our next lesson will focus on the Motivational Gift of Exhortation.

Personal Study Questions:

1. Can you name a person in the bible who was called "son of encouragement "?

2. Can you list at least 4 attributes or traits of that person who demonstrated the Motivational Gift of Exhortation?

Lesson 7

The Motivational Gift of Exhortation

The 7 Motivational Spiritual Gifts are found in Romans 12: 1-8

Prophecy

Serving (hospitality, ministry of helps)

Giving

Administration (to lead; rule; organize)

Exhortation

Teaching

Mercy (Compassion)

Review~ Ruminate ~ Commit to Memory

Let's review what we have learned thus far. The **Motivational Gift of Prophecy** is referred to as the **"eye of the body"**; the **Motivational Gift of Serving** is referred to as the **"hand of the body"** and the **Motivational Gift of Giving** is referred to as the **"arm of the body"**. The **Motivational Gift of Administration** is referred to as the **"shoulder of the body "**. In this lesson we are going to look at the **Motivational Gift of Exhortation** which is referred to as **"the mouth of the body"**. If you know individuals who operate or demonstrate this gift, you know that they have a lot to say, they talk a lot. **God has given them oratorical skills that are phenomenal.**

The Motivational Gift of Exhortation - The mouth of the Body

Don and Katie Fortune's observation reveals that teachers aim for your head, while the exhorter aims for your heart. The exhorter wants to impart information that will not only impact your life but wants that same information utilized effectively in your life. They are interested in practical life applications. What I found interesting was the **Greek word paraklesis means "a calling to one's side to aid "denoting both exhortation and encouragement**. The Holy Spirit is known as a Paraclete, a Helper and Comforter which is taken from this root word paraklesis. You will find Exhorters in ministries that involve counseling, teaching or discipling.

Attributes or Traits of this type of Individual

- Exhorters love to counsel people.
- They demand a lot from themselves and others.
- They encourage others to live up to their fullest potential (encouraging individuals to live victorious lives).
- They develop action plans for individuals to attain personal growth.
- They are outstanding communicators.
- They have the ability to see how tribulations can produce maturity (believe all things will work together, that test and trials will produce a perfect work which will leave the individual lacking nothing).
- They are very optimistic and well-liked by others.
- They accept people for who they are without judgement.
- Their lifestyle is their preferred tool for evangelism or witnessing.
- They waste no time in resolving conflicts.
- They need an outlet to air out ideas or thoughts.
- They make decisions quickly and easily.
- They enjoy reading or sharing truth that has a practical application.
- They have the ability to give constructive and helpful advice.

Review of Personal Study Questions:

1. Can you name a person in the bible who was called "son of encouragement "?

2. Can you list at least 4 attributes or traits of that person who demonstrated the Motivational Gift of Exhortation?

Old Testament Example:

Aaron- Aaron had excellent oratorical abilities. Moses mentions his eloquence of speech in Exodus chapter 3 and 7. In Exodus chapters 4-12- It is implied that Aaron was not only relied upon because of his oratorical abilities but as an advisor to Moses. In, <u>Exodus 17: 10-12</u> Aaron stood beside Moses (along with Hur) to uphold Moses arms during the battle against the Amalekites. This symbolic gesture implies the shared responsibility of managing the children of Israel. We should also note that later Aaron was consecrated and set in the office as High Priest.

New Testament Examples: <u>Acts 4:36</u> (cjb)

Thus **Yosef, (Joseph)** whom the **emissaries (apostles) called Bar-Nabba (which means "the Exhorter")**, a Levite and a native of Cyprus. Because Joseph was known as an encourager, the apostles gave him the name Barnabus which meant "son of encouragement".

It is interesting to note that when Paul (Saul) at the time had come to Jerusalem, he tried to join the disciples, but they were afraid of him and did not believe that he was a true disciple because of his past. They were uncertain that Saul's conversion was authentic.

Acts 9:27- However, Bar-Nabba got hold of him and took him to the emissaries. He told them how Sha'ul had seen the Lord while traveling, that the Lord had spoken to him, and how in Dammesek Sha'ul had spoken out boldly in the name of Yeshua. **28** So he remained with them and went all over Yerushalayim continuing to speak out boldly in the name of the Lord.

- One of the most prominent attributes of an individual who demonstrates the **Motivational Gift of Exhortation** is they accept people for who they are without judgement. Barnabus is not concerned about Saul's past he is optimistic about Saul's future. It is with great anticipation that Barnabus sort of mentors Saul in his early ministry. They are found working alongside of each other in ministry encouraging the various early churches. We can only assume that Barnabus played an intricate role in helping Paul to become the awesome Apostle and prolific Teacher of his time. Paul too, can be viewed as one whose motivational gift was "Exhortation". We can look to his letters to the Churches of Galatia, Ephesus and Colosse. There are too many to list so we are going to focus on Barnabus. You may read <u>Acts chapters 12 – 15.</u>

Acts 11:22-26 News of this reached the ears of the Messianic community in Yerushalayim, and they sent Bar-Nabba to Antioch.

<u>VERSE 22</u> **Barnabus was dispatched to Antioch**

23 (amplified) *When he arrived and saw what grace **(favor)** God was bestowing upon them, he was full of joy and he continuously exhorted **(warned, urged and encouraged)** them all to cleave unto and remain faithful to and devoted to the Lord with **(resolute and steady)** purpose of heart.*

VERSE 23 Barnabus exhorts the people to be faithful, demonstrates his practical faith; is very optimistic and joyful and expects a lot from the group.

24 *for he was a good man, full of and controlled by the Ruach HaKodesh and full of faith and trust.*

 VERSE 24 He focuses on the people; he has a life of witness, living by example.

25 *Then Bar-Nabba went off to Tarsus to look for Sha'ul;*

VERSE 25 He does not judge Paul but embraces him. He took an interest in developing not only a relationship but help shaped the ministry gifts in Paul.

26 *and when he found him, he brought him to Antioch. They met with the congregation there for a whole year and taught a sizeable crowd. Also it was in Antioch that the **talmidim (disciples)** for the first time were called "Messianic." **(Christian)***

VERSE 26 Barnabus instructs and counsels the people to apply truth and live them out in everyday life. By being committed to the task for one year would indicate his focus was on the development of the early church.

Misunderstandings of the Motivational Gift of Administration

- They will interrupt a conversation in order to make a point or give advice or opinion (they are not unaware of this most of the time).
- Will take scripture out of context to support their opinions or to make a point.
- They can fall into a trap of giving "pat" answers. One size fits all mentality (when counseling or giving advice if the problems are similar they will use the same methodology of resolve).
- They are very opinionated. They tend to be bossy. (Their mouth gets ahead of their mind).
- Can become overly self-confident (they believe they have the answer for every problem and situation).

Our next lesson will focus on the Motivational Gift of Teaching.

Personal Study Question:

Can you name a husband and wife who may have demonstrated the Motivational Gift of Teaching while establishing the early church?

Lesson 8

The Motivational Gift of Teaching

The 7 Motivational Spiritual Gifts are found in Romans 12: 1-8

Prophecy

Serving (hospitality, ministry of helps)

Giving

Administration (to lead; rule; organize)

Exhortation

Teaching

Mercy (Compassion)

As we have done in previous lessons let's take some time to review what we have discovered regarding motivational gifts. We have learned that the **Motivational Gift of** P**rophecy** is referred to as the **"eye of the body"**; the **Motivational Gift of Serving** is referred to as the **"hand of the body"**. The **Motivational Gift of Giving** is referred to as the **"arm of the body"**; the **Motivational Gift of Administration** is referred to as the **"shoulder of the body "**and the **Motivational Gift of Exhortation** is referred to as **"the mouth of the body"**. In this lesson we are going to look at the **Motivational Gift of Teaching** which is referred to as the **"mind of the body"**. To quote Don and Katie Fortune, **"Teachers are exceptionally gifted and intelligent. They are always asking questions. They want to know the basis for everything and they will search until the facts convince them that something is true."**

The Motivational Gift of Teaching - The mind of the Body

Remember teachers aim for your head. They want you to have a paradigm shift. They challenge you to renew your mind based upon truth presented to you, truth that you hear and truth that you embrace.

When we studied the nine spiritual gifts of the Holy Spirit we noted that there were:

Three Spoken gifts- diverse tongues, interpretation of tongues and prophecy.

Three Power gifts- healing; working of miracles and faith.

Three Revelatory gifts- word of wisdom; word of knowledge; discerning of spirits.

Motivational gifts are categorically defined much in the same way. **We have four speaking gifts and three serving gifts.** Let me make this plain. The Motivational Gift of Prophecy, which is the "eye of the body", **uses speech** to make God's will known. The Gift of Exhortation which is the "mouth of the body" **uses speech** to encourage and exhort. The Motivational Gift of Administration which is the "shoulder of the body" **uses speech** in order to lead or facilitate organization within the body. Lastly, the teacher which is the "mind of the body" **uses speech** in order to teach. **These four gifts are then referred to as "the speaking gifts". The Motivational Gift of Mercy or compassion, is the "heart of the body"; the Motivational Gift of Giving, which is the "arm of the body" and the Motivational Gift of Serving or ministry of helps which is the "hand of the body" are all referred to as "the three serving gifts and function in supportive roles behind the scenes.**

What we have then is a body that is depicted spiritually and naturally functioning as **"one interdependent body"** that is led by the Holy

Spirit's Spoken Word, Power and Revelation that **communicates and serves harmoniously** with one another.

Attributes or Traits of this type of Individual

- They have a way of presenting truth simply, systematically and logically.
- They have a need to validate truth by researching facts.
- They love to study.
- They are "wordsmiths" and are fascinated with the origins of words.
- They deter from non-biblically based illustrations.
- The Bible is their ultimate Authority.
- They believe that the "teaching gift" is foundational to other gifts.
- They prefer teaching believers or new converts over evangelistic outreach.
- They have sharp intellectual abilities.
- They are self-motivated and self-disciplined.
- They like to challenge or test other teachers.

Old Testament Example:

Ezra- Ezra 7: 6-14, 25 (cjb)

*6 this 'Ezra went up from **Bavel (Babylon)**. **He was a scribe, expert (skilled)** in the Torah of Moshe, which ADONAI the God of Isra'el had given; and the king granted him everything he asked for, since the hand of ADONAI his God was on him. 10 For 'Ezra had **set his heart on studying and practicing** the Torah of ADONAI and **teaching Isra'el the laws and rulings**. 11 Here is the letter that King Artach'shashta gave 'Ezra the **cohen (priest)** and Torah-teacher, the student of matters relating to ADONAI's **mitzvot (commandment)** and his laws for Isra'el: 14 You are being sent by the king and his seven counselors to inquire how the law of your God, of which you have expert knowledge, is being applied in Y'hudah and Yerushalayim.*

*25 "And you, 'Ezra, **making use of the wisdom you have from your God**, are to appoint magistrates and judges to judge all the people in the territory beyond the River, that is, all who know the laws of your God; **and you are to teach those who don't know them.***

Review of Personal Study Question:

Can you name a husband and wife who may have demonstrated the Motivational Gift of Teaching while establishing the early church?

New Testament Examples:

- Aquila and Priscilla – Acts 18: 1-3; 18,19;24-28; Romans 16: 1-5; 1 Corinthians 16:19; 2 Timothy 4:19
- Apollos- Acts 18 – (nas)

<u>Acts 28:24-28</u> Now *a Jew named Apollos, an Alexandrian by birth, an eloquent man, came to Ephesus; and he was mighty in the Scriptures. 25 This man had been instructed in the way of the Lord; and being fervent in spirit, he was speaking and teaching accurately the things concerning Jesus, being acquainted only with the baptism of John; 26 and he began to speak out boldly in the synagogue. But when Priscilla and Aquila heard him, they took him aside and explained to him the way of God more accurately. 27 And when he wanted to go across to Achaia, the brethren encouraged him and wrote to the disciples to welcome him; and when he had arrived, he greatly helped those who had believed through grace, 28 for he powerfully refuted the Jews in public, demonstrating by the Scriptures that Jesus was the Christ.*

<u>1 Corinthians 3:1-6</u> *As for me, brothers, I couldn't talk to you as spiritual people but as worldly people, as babies, so far as experience with the Messiah is concerned. 2 I gave you milk, not solid food, because you were not yet ready for it. But you aren't ready for it now either! 3 For you are still*

worldly! Isn't it obvious from all the jealousy and quarrelling among you that you are worldly and living by merely human standards? 4 For when one says, "I follow Sha'ul" and another, "I follow Apollos," aren't you being merely human? 5 After all, what is Apollos? What is Sha'ul? Only servants through whom you came to trust. Indeed, it was the Lord who brought you to trust through one of us or through another. 6 I planted the seed, and Apollos watered it, but it was God who made it grow.

In these verses of scripture we clearly see the attributes of Apollos' teaching gift. His intellect and logic; his bible focus; his accuracy regarding scripture about what he knows; his strong convictions relative to his teachings and his own teachable spirit are all on display.

Paul – who walked in the office as an Apostle, had the motivational gift of Exhortation and Teaching. Teaching was his most dominate motivational gift. It is stated by scholars that Paul records the most systematic presentation of doctrine in the Bible. His education reflected that of teacher, lawyer and minister in his Jewish upbringing. He was well versed in scripture studying under the tutelage of Gamaliel a celebrated Rabbi. After Paul's conversion he spent three years in Arabia where he was a dedicated student having received revelation of Jesus Christ by the Holy Spirit. <u>Galatians 1:11-17</u>.

<u>**Misunderstandings of the Motivational Gift of Administration**</u>

- They may be dogmatic or legalistic.
- They may appear to be full of pride because of their intellectual prowess.
- Their study gift may appear to come from intellect rather than the Holy Spirit.
- They tend to neglect the practical application preferring to highlight the scriptural truth.

- Too many details of their study may be unnecessary to the listener or the student.

In our next lesson we will focus on the last gift which is the Motivational Gift of "Mercy or Compassion ".

Personal Study Questions:

1. How many times is it mentioned that Jesus was moved or displayed "compassion" in the New Testament scriptures?

2. What parable does Jesus use to describe the attributes of compassion and where is it found in scripture?

Lesson 9

The Motivational Gift of Mercy

The 7 Motivational Spiritual Gifts are found in Romans 12: 1-8

Prophecy

Serving (hospitality, ministry of helps)

Giving

Administration (to lead; rule; organize)

Exhortation

Teaching

Mercy (Compassion)

By way of review we have discovered that the **motivational gift of prophecy** is referred to as the **"eye of the body"; the motivational gift of serving** is referred to as the **"hand of the body"**. The **motivational gift of giving** is referred to as the **"arm of the body"; the motivational gift of administration** is referred to as the **"shoulder of the body"** and the **motivational gift of exhortation** is referred to as **"the mouth of the body";** and **the motivational gift of teaching** is referred to as the **"mind of the body"**. In this lesson we are going to talk about a gift that is referred to as the **"heart of the body "**which is the **motivational gift of mercy or compassion.**

<u>The Motivational Gift of Mercy (Compassion) - The heart of the Body</u>

Individuals who demonstrate this gift are generally people who are guided by their hearts and are drawn to people who are in need physically and spiritually. When it comes to relationships and interactions with others their genuine concern and care are evident.

Because they feel deeply and love wholeheartedly, the loving nature of God is revealed by their kindness. The individual that is motivated by compassion or mercy is genuinely sorry that you are hurting and they will hurt with you. They will walk you through "hurtful situations" until the hurt is gone.

2 Thessalonians 3:5 says *"May the Lord direct your hearts into God's love and the perseverance which the Messiah gives "*which is not only a lifestyle but a befitting scripture for the individual who is totally motivated by compassion and or mercy.

Attributes or Traits of this type of Individual

They have a tremendous capacity to demonstrate unconditional love.

They only see the best in others. They are non-critical and non-judgmental.

They can detect ones emotional condition.

They are always attracted to hurting people.

They take action to remove the hurt or distress of others.

They are peacemakers.

They can detect when motives are wrong or insincere.

They are drawn to others who demonstrate the gift of compassion or mercy.

They do not like confrontation or conflict.

They are always doing things that are thoughtful.

They are very trusting of people.

They are governed by their heart and their emotions.

They are intercessors- praying with abandonment and freely expressing their emotions.

<u>Old Testament Example</u>:

Ruth

***<u>Ruth 1: 16-18 (cjb)</u>** But Rut said, "Don't press me to leave you and stop following you; for wherever you go, I will go; and wherever you stay, I will stay. Your people will be my people and your God will be my God. **17** Where you die, I will die; and there I will be buried. May ADONAI bring terrible curses on me, and worse ones as well, if anything but death separates you and me." **18** When Na'omi saw that she was determined to go with her, she said no more to her.*

<u>Verse 16-18</u> We observe Ruth's compassion toward her mother-in-law for the loss of Naomi's husband and two sons, in spite of her own grief of losing her husband. What a perspective! She is determined to take action to remove the grief of Naomi by staying by her side until death separates them. By this action of kindness she also demonstrates to us what unconditional love looks like.

<u>Ruth 2: 10-11 (cjb)</u> *She fell on her face, prostrating herself, and said to him, "Why are you showing me such favor? Why are you paying attention to me? After all, I'm only a foreigner." **11** Bo'az answered her, **"I've heard the whole story, everything you've done for your mother-in-law since your husband died, including how you left your father and mother and the land you were born in to come to a people about whom you knew nothing beforehand.***

<u>Verses: 10, 11</u> Ruth is known for her compassion and kindness among a people to whom she is a stranger. Her compassion; kindness and good deeds toward her mother-in-law speaks volumes about her character and the type of woman she was.

Review of Personal Study Questions:

Question 1: **How many times is it mentioned that Jesus was moved or displayed mercy or compassion?**

Answer: New Testament reveals 10 times- Matthew 9:36; Matthew 14:14; Matthew 15:32; Matthew 18:33; Matthew 20:34; Mark 1:41; Mark 5:19; Mark 6:34; Mark 8:2; Luke 7:13.

Question 2: **What parable does Jesus use to describe the characteristics of mercy or compassion and where is it found in scripture?**

Answer: The Good Samaritan found in Luke 10: 25-37

New Testament Example:

The Good Samaritan

Luke 10:25-35 (cjb) *An expert in Torah stood up to try and trap him by asking, "Rabbi, what should I do to obtain eternal life?" 26 But Yeshua said to him, "What is written in the Torah? How do you read it?" 27 He answered, "You are to love ADONAI your God with all your heart, with all your soul, with all your strength and with all your understanding; and your neighbor as yourself." 28 "That's the right answer," Yeshua said. "Do this, and you will have life?" 29 But he, wanting to justify himself, said to Yeshua, "And who is my `neighbor'?" 30 Taking up the question, Yeshua said: "A man was going down from Yerushalayim to Yericho when he was attacked by robbers. They stripped him naked and beat him up, then went off, leaving him half dead. 31 By coincidence, a* **cohen (priest)** *was going down on that road; but when he saw him, he passed by on the other side.*

Verse 31 Compassion is not found in the actions of the priest, a religious leader, and a man of the cloth, who should have had compassion.

32 *Likewise a Levi who reached the place and saw him also passed by on the other side.*

<u>Verse 32</u> The Levite is also void of compassion as well. Again he is a Levitical priest, a "man of God", and we find no kindness of empathy coming from this individual.

33 *"But a man from Shomron who was traveling came upon him; and when he saw him, he was moved with compassion.*

<u>Verse 33</u> The love of this individual comes from the heart. He not only takes care of the injured person, he anticipates any emotional distress that might be revealed as the person recovers.

34 *So he went up to him, put oil and wine on his wounds and bandaged them. Then he set him on his own donkey, brought him to an inn and took care of him.*

<u>Verse 34</u> Action is taken to remove the hurt emotionally and physically. The Good Samaritan breaks through barriers that prevailed between two ethnically prejudiced cultures in order to render aid.

35 *The next day, he took out two days' wages, gave them to the innkeeper and said, `Look after him; and if you spend more than this, I'll pay you back when I return.'*

<u>Verse 35 </u>He places his trust in the Innkeeper to continue the care the injured man had receive and assured the Innkeeper of any future payment.

Misunderstandings of the Motivational Gift of Mercy or Compassion

- Their natural affection can be misinterpreted by the opposite sex.
- They are indecisive. They have a hard time coming to decisions.
- They are quick to come to the aid of an offended person.
- They take up the causes of the "under dog".
- They are easily hurt or offended themselves.
- They take on the burden of others.
- Their "empathy scale" can get out of balance which renders them ineffective.

I want to leave you with this analogy that comes from Don and Katie Fortune's book "Discover Your God- Given Gifts. " Suppose you have seven people over for dinner and each just happens to have a different motivational gift. You are bringing three salad plates to the table when one slips from your grip and crashes to the floor, scattering bits of glass and salad in one big mess. How will each person react they ask?

The one with the gift of prophecy will say "That's what happens when you try to carry too many plates". The ministry of helps or server will say "I'll clean it up." The teacher will say, "The reason you dropped those plates was because it was not balanced properly". The one with the gift of exhortation will say, "Next time, let someone help you carry the plates." The giver will say, I'll be glad to help make another salad". The administrator will say "John get the broom and dustpan. Sally, bring the mop and Marie help me fix another salad". The person who is motivated by compassion will say "Don't feel embarrassed it could have happened to anyone".

Learn to live with your giftedness and recognize and accept the "gifts" of others.

Section 4

THE FRUITS OF CHARACTER

Lesson 1

The Fruits of Character

Question: What is character?

Question: What does the Bible have to say about character?

Question: What are the fruits of character?

Question: How do we develop character?

What is Character?

There are many definitions regarding character found in the dictionary; such as good moral or ethical qualities; one's reputation and the aggregate of features and traits that form the individual nature of some person or thing. An account of the qualities or peculiarities of a person and finally an inscription that is engraved or etched in one's persona. I like the latter definition because it aligns with the Bibles view of character.

What does the Bible have to say about character?

The Bible uses different terminology in both the Old Testament and in the New Testament to describe what character might look like. There are several young men like Joseph and Daniel and a few women that exhibited such character traits. Take for instance.

In **Ruth 3:11** the Complete Jewish Bible translation speaks of Ruth's "good character" *And now, my daughter, don't be afraid. I will do for you everything you say, for all the city leaders among my people know that you are a woman of good character.*

But the New King James version speaks of Ruth's "virtuous qualities" *And now, my daughter, do not fear. I will do for you all that you request for all the people of my town know that you are a virtuous woman.*

In both of these translations it is obvious that Ruth's conduct or the way she carried herself was noticeable by all who came into contact with her. She left an impression on those she encountered. Her good character gained her favor!

In **Daniel 6: 2-4** the Complete Jewish Bible translation speaks of Daniels **"extraordinary spirit"**. Verse 1, 2 tells us that there were *three chiefs over the viceroys, of whom Dani'el was one, so that these viceroys could be responsible to them and so that the king's interests would be safeguarded. 3 But because an extraordinary spirit was in this Dani'el, he so distinguished himself above the other chiefs and the viceroys that the king considered putting him in charge of the whole kingdom. 4 The other chiefs and the viceroys tried to find a cause for complaint against Dani'el in regard to how he performed his governing duties, but they could find nothing to complain about, no fault; on the contrary, because he was so faithful, not a single instance of negligence or faulty administration could be found.*

The New Kings James version speaks of Daniel's **" excellent spirit "** *2 and over these, three governors, of whom Daniel was one, that the satraps might give account to them, so that the king would suffer no loss. 3 Then this Daniel distinguished himself above the governors and satraps, because an excellent spirit was in him; and the king gave thought to setting him over the whole realm. 4 So the governors and satraps sought to find some charge against Daniel concerning the kingdom; but they could find no charge or fault, because he was faithful; nor was there any error or fault found in him.*

Daniel conducted the king's business affairs with integrity and his lifestyle was beyond reproach. His co-workers could not find anything in his character that they could use against him. Because Daniel had such an excellent spirit he found favor with the King who decided he deserved to be promoted!

There are similar examples in the New Testament.

One example is found in **Philippians 2: 19-22** the Complete Jewish Bible speaks of Timothy's "caring and unselfish" demeanor. *But I hope* *in the Lord Yeshua to send Timothy to you shortly, so that I too may be cheered by knowing how you are doing. 20 I have no one who compares with him, who will care so sincerely for your welfare - 21 people all put their own interests ahead of the Messiah Yeshua's. 22 But you know his character, that like a child with his father he slaved with me to advance the Good News.*

But the New King James version speaks of his "proven character". *But I trust in the Lord Jesus to send Timothy to you shortly, that I also may be encouraged when I know your state. 20 For I have no one like-minded, who will sincerely care for your state. 21 For all seek their own, not the things which are of Christ Jesus. 22 But you know his proven character, that as a son with his father he served with me in the gospel.*

Timothy is highly spoken well of by his Mentor, the Apostle Paul. His demeanor and work ethic was consistent and observed by others whom Paul is speaking.

Personal Study Read **Acts 17:11** and **Acts 6:1-15** in several translations and identify features or traits that reference those specific individual's character.

The men and woman we mentioned in this lesson all portrayed traits about their personality that set them apart and exemplified the character of Christ in their lives. They were not just Sunday morning believers or Wednesday night bible study goers; they exhibited godly character in their everyday lives. They lived "in the world" but were not part "of the world". The world system; social settings or work environments to which they belonged could not change or influence who they were or how they lived.

What are the fruits of character?

The fruits of character are born out of a relationship with the Holy Spirit and we call them the **fruit of the Spirit**. When we walk and live in the Spirit we learn to disallow the old nature or the deeds of the old nature to dominate our way of living or thinking. The Holy Spirit, **Ruach HaKodesh** is our Helper and therefore helps us in our transformation process. He reminds us; convicts us and corrects us with the Word of God to conform us into the image of Christ. In return, we must be trusting and totally yielded to Him.

A fruit tree bears fruit which resembles the seed that was planted and is nourished by the root system. There has to be a healthy root system in order for the fruit to be without blemishes, flaws or deficiencies. The Word of God is the seed and the Holy Spirit, **Ruach HaKodesh** is the root system.

Look at what the bible says about the **fruit of the Spirit** found in **Galatians 5:22, 23.** Notice I said look at the **"fruit"** not **"fruits"** of the Holy Spirit. The Holy Spirit produces the nine fold fruit which is all encompassing and characterizes those who walk in the Spirit. They are Love, Joy, Peace, Longsuffering (patience), Kindness, Goodness, Faithfulness, Gentleness, Self-Control (temperance).

Personal Study Using the New King James version of the Bible, review the scriptures associated with the fruit listed below. How can they be applied in your current circumstances? What fruit do you need to develop further based on these scriptures.

Love – 1 John 4:16, John 15:13

Joy – Nehemiah 8:10, Hebrews 12:2

Peace – Philippians 4: 6, 7; Romans 15:13

Longsuffering – Colossians 1:11, Ephesians 4

Kindness - Ruth 3:10, Joshua 2:12

Goodness – 2 Thessalonians 1:11, Ephesians 5:9

Faithfulness – Isaiah 25:1, 2 Chronicles 31:18

Gentleness – Philippians 4:5, 2 Samuel 22:36

Self-Control - 1 Thessalonians 4: 1-8, 1 Corinthians 6:12-20

How do we develop character?

<u>Answer</u>: There are 2 scripture keys to developing character.

<u>Galatians 2:20</u> – Crucify the flesh and let Christ live in your life through faith.

<u>Romans 8: 12-17</u>- Allow the Holy Spirit to lead and guide you every day.

<u>2 Peter 1: 5-8</u> has this to say about spiritual growth and character development.

Grace and peace be multiplied to you in the knowledge of God and of Jesus our Lord, 3 as His divine power has given to us all things that pertain to life and godliness, through the knowledge of Him who called us by glory and virtue, 4 by which have been given to us exceedingly great and precious promises, that through these you may be partakers of the divine nature, having escaped the corruption that is in the world through lust. 5 But also for this very reason, giving all diligence, add to your faith virtue, to virtue knowledge, 6 to knowledge self-control, to self-control perseverance, to perseverance godliness, 7 to godliness brotherly kindness, and to brotherly kindness love. 8 For if these things are yours and abound, you will be neither barren nor unfruitful in the knowledge of our Lord Jesus Christ.

KEEP GROWING!

Lesson 2

Love is the Greatest

The Bible is the greatest **"Love Story"** ever written. From the beginning, God displayed His *Love* for mankind when He created a beautiful habitation called Eden which when translated means "pleasure and delight". Therefore, God's original plan was for mankind to dwell in a place that would be pleasurable and delightful all the days of their lives. God spared nothing for His creation. He created everything imaginable from precious metals and gemstones to plants, herbs and animals. And He gave them power and dominion over all that He created so they could enjoy a stress free life of abundance and pleasure, because **He loved them.**

In reality Adam and Eve chose to display dissatisfaction with **what had been created, but forbidden and withheld from them,** because they disobeyed God's instructions. Because of God's **unconditional love** for His creation He rescued them from a life totally separated from Him. The Bible tells us before the foundation of the earth Christ died for all of mankind. <u>1 Peter 1:20</u>. God said *"no greater love than this that a man should lay down his life for another"*, Jesus was that Man. <u>John 15:13</u>. *For God so loved the world that He gave His only begotten Son.* <u>John 3:16.</u> Again, proving *His Love* for His creation.

God has never withheld His *Love* from His children. **God is Love!** When the children of Israel time and time again disobeyed Him, God lovingly restored them back to fellowshipping with Him. He reminded them that He loved them with an **"everlasting love"**, therefore with lovingkindness He drew them back to Himself. He called them a holy people, a chosen people to Himself, a special treasure above all people on the earth. He did not set His love, nor chose them because they were great in number, He chose them because **He loved** them and would keep His covenant with their forefathers. **Deuteronomy 7:7, 8**. I hope I have painted on the canvas of your mind the kind of **Love** that would manifest regardless of their spiritual condition. This is the same kind of *Love* that He demonstrates towards me and you. **1 John 3: 1** says, *"See what love the Father has lavished on us in letting us be called God's children! For that is what we are. The reason the world does not know us is that it has not known him"*.

With this kind of *Love* on display throughout the Bible it is clear that we too should endeavor to exhibit that same kind of **Love** in our own lives without hesitation toward others. **Kenneth Copeland says to "walk in Love is to walk in the highest spiritual realm there is". In addition to that thought, I say to walk in Love is a personal choice and requires a commitment.**

Personal Study What was the greatest commandment given to us? Read the following scriptures and write out your answers.

Matthew 5:43

Matthew 19:19

Mark 12: 31

Galatians 5:14

James 2:8

The A, B, C's of Love

Apply the Golden Rule whenever hatred stirs up strife because love covers all sin according to **Proverbs 10:12**. The Bible also says he who covers a transgression that individual seeks love. **Proverbs 17:9.**

Become acquainted with the **Love of God** and rely on **His Love**. Whenever we demonstrate a life of love, God lives in us.

Commit to live by **1 Corinthians 13** (cjb)

1 I may speak in the tongues of men, even angels; but if I lack love, I have become merely blaring brass or a cymbal clanging.

2 I may have the gift of prophecy, I may fathom all mysteries, know all things, have all faith - enough to move mountains; but if I lack love, I am nothing.

3 I may give away everything that I own, I may even hand over my body to be burned; but if I lack love, I gain nothing.

4 Love is patient and kind, not jealous, not boastful,

5 not proud, rude or selfish, not easily angered, and it keeps no record of wrongs.

6 Love does not gloat over other people's sins but takes its delight in the truth.

7 Love always bears up, always trusts, always hopes, always endures.

8 Love never ends; but prophecies will pass, tongues will cease, knowledge will pass.

9 For our knowledge is partial, and our prophecy partial;

10 but when the perfect comes, the partial will pass.

11 When I was a child, I spoke like a child, thought like a child, argued like a child; now that I have become a man, I have finished with childish ways.

12 For now we see obscurely in a mirror, but then it will be face to face. Now I know partly; then I will know fully, just as God has fully known me.

13 But for now, three things last trust, hope, love; and the <u>greatest of these is love</u>.

Demonstrate daily **John 15:13** (cjb)

No one has greater love than a person who lays down his life for his friends.

<u>Endeavor</u> to prioritize <u>Mark12:30, 31</u> (cjb)

30 and you are to love ADONAI your God with all your heart, with all your soul, with all your understanding and with all your strength.'

31 The second is this: `You are to love your neighbor as yourself.' There is no other mitzvah greater than these."

<u>Finally</u> our greatest goal should be to do all things in Love through Jesus Christ!

Section 5

MOTIVATIONAL GIFT ASSESSMENT SURVEY

Motivational Survey Questions	5	3	1	0
1. I am more comfortable demonstrating love in deeds rather than in than words.				
2. I am drawn to help people in times of trouble.				
3. I have a great desire to see the Word become flesh in others.				
4. I am alert to valid needs that I fear others will overlook.				
5. I have a strong desire to see others repent.				
6. I experience great pleasure in carrying out the details of a long-range assignment.				
7. The idea of studying just for the sake of studying is very appealing to me.				
8. I become concerned when others believe I do not want to help with the practical work in a concrete way.				
9. I am often able to discern the true motives of people.				
10. I encourage others to "go through" so that Christ can be fully formed in them.				
11. I am overjoyed when my gift is an answer to prayer for a person.				
12. When talking and dealing with people, I am frank, direct and very persuasive.				
13. I am aware of the resources which are necessary and available to complete a task.				
14. I remember the likes and dislikes of those whom I serve.				
15. Finding help for people who are in crisis situations is something I take pleasure in doing.				
16. Using relational skills in counseling has been an important part of my Christian experience.				

Motivational Survey Questions	5	3	1	0
17. I love and enjoy giving my material possessions to others.				
18. The ability to see the results of something and communicate it is relevant to my life.				
19. Determining priorities and organizing the resources to meet them is something I enjoy doing.				
20. I enjoy planning and preparing to lead others in a learning experience.				
21. I enjoy helping people who are ill on a continuous basis.				
22. I enjoy looking for people with needs and finding ways to help them.				
23. I frequently find myself counseling with people and trying to get them to do what the Word says.				
24. I like to share whatever resources I have and find joy in identifying with those who are doing a work I support.				
25. I find pleasure in publicly declaring what God is doing in and through His Word.				
26. I believe a person should put great emphasis on the accuracy of the Word.				
27. Whenever there is a job to do, I will do it and even volunteer to do extra work to see it completed.				
28. I enjoy collaborating with others who are sensitive to people's needs.				
29. I love to give without anybody knowing when I give to valid ministries and projects.				
30. When in my presence people are usually brought to conviction and fall to their knees in repentance and humility.				
31. I like to help others develop and excel in their ministries.				
32. I delight in doing research in order to validate truth.				

Motivational Survey Questions	5	3	1	0
33. I sometimes get side tracked with the needs of others rather than follow the leader's directions.				
34. I have a greater concern for mental distress than physical distress in others.				
35. I am sometimes accused of being more interested in the process or the steps of action rather than in the person's feelings.				
36. I have had my intimate relationships hampered because of my public boldness in proclaiming what I think is truth.				
37. I tend to assume responsibility for leadership roles if no designated leader is present.				
38. I avoid using non-scriptural resources to illustrate my points.				
39. Serving the needs of others is more important to me than having my needs met.				
40. I can spot insincerity and will be disturbed when my work is not sincerely appreciated.				
41. I avoid being firm unless I can see how it brings benefits.				
42. I am grieved when teaching is high and lofty without practical application.				
43. Others are encouraged to give by my generous gift giving.				
44. I experience tears and get emotional when other are brought to true repentance.				
45. I am strongly motivated to organize whatever I am responsible for.				
46. I find myself often involved in a lot of activities because saying no is hard for me.				
47. I am very sensitive to the words and actions of others who might cause harm or injury.				
48. I like to give step by step directions to those whom I am ministering.				

Motivational Survey Questions	5	3	1	0
49. I am very concerned that my gift be of high quality at all times.				
50. I have a dependency on scriptural truth in order to validate authority.				
51. I have the ability to know what can and cannot be delegated.				
52. I have a greater joy in research than in presenting lessons.				
53. I always feel compassion within myself when there is a need.				
54. I find myself wanting to be a strengthener and or a comforter to others when they are in need.				
55. The giving of myself to others is one of the most exciting experiences of my life.				
56. I often have an "insight" or intuitive sense about people and situations as they really are before God.				
57. I usually delegate those things which are able to be delegated and does only that which is necessary.				
58. I have a need or desire to tie the Old Testament and the New Testament together in teaching.				
59. I am willing to endure reactions from workers in order to accomplish the ultimate task.				
60. I sometimes find myself going into too many details for my listeners when I am sharing.				
61. Teachings that are taught systematically appeal to me.				
62. Teachings that are taught systematically appeal to me.				

In the spaces below enter the numerical values of each of your responses next to the number of the corresponding statement on the survey for spiritual gifts.

	Serve	Mercy	Exhort	Give	Prophecy	Admin	Teach
	1	2	3	4	5	6	7
	8	9	10	11	12	13	14
	15	16	17	18	19	20	21
	22	23	24	25	26	27	28
	29	30	31	32	33	34	35
	36	37	38	39	40	41	42
	43	44	45	46	47	48	49
	50	51	52	53	54	55	56
	57	58	59	60	61	62	63
Total							
Average							
Ranks							

About Ezra Ministries

Ezra Ministries, Inc. is a 501(c)(3) nonprofit organization and Christian ministry that believes in ministering the Word of God to the whole person, Spirit, Soul and Body to heal the brokenhearted and proclaim liberty to those who are held captive in abusive relationships. Our award winning "Inner Healing" classes equip and empower individuals to identify the wounds, bruises and the lies to embrace the Truth of God's Word to live their best life. We partner with community organizations and churches to provide training workshops, retreats, and conferences which promote healthy relationships.

Other Books & Ministry Resources
Pretty Woman, Redeemed by Promise, Destined for Purpose
Living Your Best Life – Inner Healing Program
Pretty Woman "Word of Encouragement" CD
The Laws of Prosperity 3 disc set
The Laws of Seed Time and Harvest Time 4 disc set

Contact Information
Joanne M. Green
Ezra Ministries, Inc.
E-mail: ministergreen@windstream.net
Website: www.ezraministriesinc.org
Phone: 512-270-9059

References and Resources

1. Dr. Dorothy Washington, Basic Bible Principles of Bible Doctrine

2. Institute in Basic Life Principles, "What are the seven motivational gifts"?

3. Don & Katie Fortune, "Discover Your God-Given Gifts" 1987, 2009, Chosen Books

Made in the USA
Coppell, TX
03 February 2020